Earth Wisdom

*Connect With Nature
and Your Inner Self*

JAN HORNFORD

 FriesenPress

One Printers Way
Altona, MB R0G 0B0
Canada

www.friesenpress.com

ISBN
978-1-03-830661-6 (Hardcover)
978-1-03-830660-9 (Paperback)
978-1-03-830662-3 (eBook)

1. *BODY, MIND & SPIRIT, GAIA & EARTH ENERGIES*

Distributed to the trade by The Ingram Book Company

Table of Contents

Introduction vii
  Journal Entry: Earth Communion x

Chapter One: Wild Wisdom 1
  Wild Wisdom Meditation 5
  Sacred Gifts 9

Chapter Two: Inner Wisdom 11
  Grounded Flow Practice 13
  Journal Entry: A Winter's Day 14
  Finding Self Love and your Inner Voice 15
  Cultivating Gratitude 17
  Grounded Flow Practice: Appreciating Beauty 17
  Accessing Emotions and Insights 18
  Uncovering Inner Guidance and Direction 20

Chapter Three: Tree Wisdom 23
  Talking to Trees 25
  Journal Entry: Dances with Trees 28
  Forest Singing 29
  Tree Spirit Guide Meditation 31

Chapter Four: Animal Wisdom 35
  Animals in Nature 35
  Animal Awareness Practice 36
  Domestic Animals 37
  Communing With Your Pet 38
  Animal Spirit Guides and Messengers 38
  Receiving Animal Messages Practice 42
  Power Animals 43

Meditation to Meet Your Power Animal 44

Journal Entry: Sandhill Crane 46

Aligning With Your Power Animal 46

Other Animal Spirit Guides 48

Chapter Five: Earth Rhythm Wisdom **51**

Inner Knowing 52

Celtic Wisdom 52

Earth Rhythm Correspondences 55

Healing Negative Associations with the Seasons 77

Chapter Six: A Spiritual Practice **79**

Connecting with the Sacred 79

Creating Your Own Altar 81

Ceremony 81

Living Intentionally 85

Final Words **91**

Journal Entry: A Summer Storm 93

A Blessing for You 94

Acknowledgements **95**

Tips for Day Hikes in Wilderness Areas **97**

Bibliography **99**

Introduction

I WANT TO TELL YOU a story of wind and water, of stars and stones, of a living wisdom that flows from the heart of Nature to the centre of your being. I want to show you how Nature can transform you, giving you peace, joy, and well-being. I want to help you discover the magic and mystery of the Earth, to travel beyond a mere enjoyment of the natural world and have a real relationship with Nature. There is an aliveness, an underlying intelligence that informs all of Nature that you can connect with and that you are a part of. You can form a vibrant, life-enhancing relationship with Nature, and Nature can connect you with your deepest, most authentic truth.

There is a wild self within you. It's the part of you that longs to live close to Nature, to walk barefoot on the grass, to feel the sun's warmth on your skin. Your wild self is your birthright. It is not something you learn or acquire. It is who you were born to be. There is an instinctive and intuitive wisdom in you that is connected, always, to Nature's wisdom.

Our ancient ancestors were deeply aware of this connection. They learned the ways of animals, the rhythm of the seasons, and the healing properties of plants. They understood that all life was sacred and connected, that everything was alive and had Spirit. They could touch the current of Spirit, the life force flowing within the natural world and within them. From Nature, they learned the cycles of birth and death, growth and rest, creation and destruction. They learned to cooperate with change rather than resist it and to be fully engaged with life. This wisdom is still alive in many cultural and spiritual traditions around the world, including Indigenous traditions. However, many of us have been dislocated in place and time from the knowledge our ancestors held. We became disconnected from the natural world and from our deepest wisdom. We lost touch with our instinctive selves in a society that honours intellect over intuition. Nature has become something to exploit—a resource rather than a wellspring—something to endure or subdue. We battle the elements; we conquer mountains; we clear forests. It feels like we are always in conflict with Nature.

Collectively, we are waking up to the fact that we can't keep taking from the Earth. During the COVID-19 pandemic, many people began to understand that Nature is vital for our physical health and mental well-being. Now, we see drought, deforestation, habitat loss, and food shortages. It is terrifying to witness these changes and easy to feel helpless or overwhelmed. I have hope. I believe in Nature's ability to heal and rebalance the ecosystems that all life depends on. I see people becoming aware that we need to live more sustainably, for ourselves and future generations, and for the good of all life on the planet. Wanting to take better care of our world is a good place to begin, but we need to do more than appreciate and care for Nature; we need to be in relationship with Nature. When we rediscover a loving and respectful relationship with Nature, we can create healing for ourselves and our planet.

It is time to rediscover the power of Nature and the wild wisdom that lives within you. Let the Earth fill your awareness and awaken your senses. Experience first-hand how alive the world is and how you are part of that aliveness. Seek the wisdom of the wild. Hear the language of plants and stones. Listen to the song of the trees. The Earth speaks to you through the wind and sky, the stars and moon, the plants and animals. Stories are written in the land and wisdom flows through the water. You carry both in your blood and bones. You need only listen.

I can hear the echo of my ancestors in my blood. My ancestors lived in places now known as the Celtic lands. They speak to me of a relationship with the land, sea, and sky. I can hear the song of my ancestors calling me to reclaim their wisdom, to rekindle my relationship with Nature. I want to help you do the same.

No one event started me on this journey. Imagine a stone pathway; each step took me deeper into the forest; every day, I found comfort and joy in the embrace of Nature, and Nature revealed more to me.

Early on in my journey, my love for the Earth and the animals and plants led me to study Zoology and eventually to earn a degree in that field. My studies helped me to understand the ways of the animals and to learn more about the ecosystems that sustain us, but I came to realize that science didn't hold all the answers.

In time, I discovered the path of Druidry and Shamanism. These traditions held ancient wisdom that was seeking to be reborn in the modern world. The world came alive again for me—full of mystery and wonder. Here were practices that made sense to me, that allowed me to weave together the biology of the animals with their Spirit strengths. Here were practices that treated all life with honour and respect and acknowledged the seen and unseen worlds. Both Shamans and Druids held tribal knowledge, communicated with the Spirits of the land, and received aid from Spirit or universal intelligence. In both traditions, one can connect with Spirit to receive wisdom, guidance, healing, protection, and power. Both open the door to a more profound understanding of reality. Both work with animal and plant spirits and have a deep awareness of the seasons, the movement of animals, and the healing plants.

The Druid path shows you how to be in communion with Nature and with the divine intelligence or Spirit that underlies and informs all life. Druidry is a practice that fosters love and respect for Nature. It helps you to develop your inner knowing, to see the world in a deeper way, and to live more fully engaged with the life around you. Druidry helps you access your creativity and enhance your potential.

Druidry is my spiritual home; it is a practice I inhabit. It is not a religion. It is a spiritual path that guides how I move in and relate to the world around me. Druidry and Shamanism do not have doctrines one must follow. These traditions offer a way of relating to all life and the divine spiritual source that manifests through the natural world. These practices teach that all life is sacred. You do not have to embrace Druidry or Shamanism to be in a loving relationship with Nature.

Nature can transform you. Nature transformed me. My change was not through the physical challenge of a wild adventure, but through the land's deep offering of grace and wisdom. I had to face uncomfortable truths. I had to conquer fears and beliefs I held. On this journey, I discovered who I truly was and how I fit into the world. I learned that the world is so much bigger than I ever imagined. Nature has been my greatest teacher and has opened a gateway to the greater life: to the seen and unseen worlds. Nature has been my path home to the inner wisdom of my soul. Being present, connected to, and in communion with the natural world healed and transformed my life.

Years before I discovered Druidry or Shamanism, I had a crisis of the heart. We can all relate to the feelings of hopelessness or despair that arise from death, divorce, job loss, or any of life's challenges. When my father died, I experienced such a moment. The following excerpt speaks to how the Earth supported me and how the Earth can help you, too.

JOURNAL ENTRY: EARTH COMMUNION

Something broke inside of me, a fault line opened my heart, and I knew my world would never be the same. Anguish engulfed me. I struggled under its weight; my breath came in ragged gasps, and tears welled up along with the pain, a geyser erupting from my broken core.

I had to get outside. Being outside was my only shelter in this personal earthquake. I wanted to hide. The bright sun blinded me as I sought a place of refuge. The only privacy in my suburban back yard was up against the side of the house, tucked in behind the rain barrel. I fell flat on my face in the soft grass and poured my pain, my sorrow, my fear into the Earth.

And something unexpected happened. I felt the Earth respond. The Earth held me. I was wrapped in the Earth's presence, held in the Earth's arms, surrounded by love and peace in my darkest moment. I was a child in my mother's arms, and I knew everything would be alright.

At that moment, I felt the Infinite, and I knew I was not alone. I felt a part of something much greater than myself and my problems...I knew I was loved and supported. Within moments, I had shifted from anguish to wonder.

The power and grace of Nature are everywhere. They are not only found in wild places or amidst mountain splendour, although you will surely find them there, but they are in your own backyard. They are in every blade of *grass and every dandelion. You will discover the love and grace of Nature in the neglected, out of the way, forgotten places within our world and within ourselves. Nature is a pure and loving presence that is always with us.* *

Nature is a cauldron that holds all the ingredients of life, including the power of transformation, regeneration, and rebirth. Nature can bring forth forgotten wisdom that lives within you, a knowing that runs deeper than who you think you are, deeper than your personality and the everyday aspects of your life. Nature can be a haven to move you through challenges, doubt, and uncertainty. What if you could experience a place of beauty and peace, full of life and energy, where you could listen to your heart's inner guidance? What would it be like to connect to something bigger than yourself?

- I believe in the healing power of Nature.

- I believe Nature is wise and can show you how to live.

- I believe a loving and respectful relationship with Nature is vital to your well-being and the well-being of the planet.

- I believe a relationship with Nature connects you to your body's wisdom and your soul's intuition.

- I believe Nature can transform your life.

Wonder and wisdom are waiting for you outside your front door. In this book, I will introduce simple practices that you can use to create a connection with the natural world. Creating a connection is not something you can read about, it is something you must experience. Many practices in this book are directed at going outside and walking in a natural area to engage with Nature. If you are not able to walk or travel to a natural landscape, it is still possible to experience Nature, to engage your senses, and to feel the life around you. The tree outside your window, an indoor plant, your pet, the sky, or a rock in your hand are all aspects of Nature that you can connect with. You can adapt many of the practices to a sitting practice, indoors or out. I encourage you to go outside, if that's possible, but if it's not, the practices and ideas in this book can still help you rekindle your relationship with Nature in a way that is right for you.

When you live connected to your deepest self and in communion with the Earth, your life is rich with meaning. This book will guide you as you reconnect with your wisdom and with the heart of Nature so you can experience more peace, joy, and love. I invite you to come with me on a journey into Nature. You will:

- Discover your body's innate wisdom and how to work with your physical senses.

- Discover how Nature can help you access your personal wisdom and intuition.

- Learn to listen to the source of life that flows through all things.

- Learn to commune with the elements, the trees, and the animals.

- Find a source of personal power through your power animal.

- Express your creativity and find inspiration in Nature.

- Create a ceremony for connection and guidance.

- Develop a spiritual practice that is uniquely your own.

- Discover how living in tune with Nature's rhythms fosters healing and transformation.

Make a commitment to go outside, see the world in a new way, and discover how Nature can transform your life.

This book is an invitation to expand your awareness and discover your deep communion with Nature. I will share with you the practices that have supported me, and I encourage you to create your own methods based on what feels right for you.

This is your journey. This is your experience. Take what has meaning to you and leave the rest. My intention is to share with you my deep love and respect for Nature and to offer a fresh perspective. Come with a sense of curiosity and an open mind. This is a journey of the body and the senses, of your heart and your inner self. It is not about acquiring knowledge; it is a voyage into your inner landscape through the outer landscape of Nature. It's not a journey in a straight line, but a spiral where life takes on a deeper meaning with each turn.

Chapter One: Wild Wisdom

NATURE IS THE TREES, the plants, the minerals, the animals, the elements of Earth, Air, Water, and Fire, all that is in the physical world. Nature invites us to fully enter this physical experience. I have always enjoyed being outside. I remember playing under the trees in my backyard. My special house was under an elm's branches. I would also stand outside in the rain, smelling the blossoms from the crab apple tree. I loved the papery bark of the birch and how the sunlight filtered through the leaves of the trees. I was always pretending to be an animal: a horse, a cougar, a deer as I moved in my "forest." There was a natural prairie behind my home, and my friends and I would play for hours in the tall grass. If I was upset or anxious, I would always find comfort with the trees in my yard. I even made up songs to sing to the trees and the prairie that I loved so much. As an adult, I would hike for days in the back country of the Rocky Mountains on backpacking trips. I have always found joy in the natural landscapes. Trees have been my friends for as long as I can remember.

It was a tree that woke me up so many years ago. My friend and I were snow-shoeing on Mount Revelstoke in British Columbia, Canada. It was a beautiful day, and we were meandering through a forest of western red cedars. These trees were magnificent! As I was trying to keep up with my triathlete friend, something unusual happened. A tree that I had already passed leapt into my consciousness. I was suddenly very aware of this individual tree. I called my friend back, and we retraced our steps until we reached this specific tree. I reached out my hand to touch the trunk. The moment my hand contacted the bark, I felt a surge of energy rush from the tree through my hand. I was infused with joy! It was like every cell of my body was ablaze with light. It was a profound experience. We stood there for a long time, just feeling the Spirit and life of this magnificent tree, soaking up this profound communion. I was never the same. That tree got me to thinking, could I talk to trees? Was there something more to life than I ever dreamt was possible? The answer is yes!

That tree opened my eyes to see Nature in a new way, to see beyond what I perceived to be my everyday reality and to consider that there might be something more to this world than meets the eye. That tree invited me to look deeper, to go beyond everything I thought I knew and to open my eyes to the greater life. I used to see just the surface of Nature. I experienced Nature through my thinking. I would spend time in Nature analyzing: the trail, the kinds of flowers I saw, looking for birds, sorting and identifying—all tasks of the mind. There is nothing wrong with this practice, it is just that we experience so much more when we start sensing Nature through our heart and all our physical senses. My encounter with that tree helped me to experience the world with my body, heart, and soul. To this day, I can still feel that tree's presence. I can tune into that tree and converse with that tree, no matter where I am in the world.

I want to help you discover this new way of looking at and being with the world. In a later chapter, we will explore tree lore and talking to trees. Right now, I want to share with you a straightforward way to begin to connect with Nature and the Spirit that lives within and around you. Divine Source, Spirit, Universal Intelligence, whatever that means to you, is expressed through us and through Nature. Begin with your physical body. There is great wisdom in your body and the physical world. Sometimes, we may think we need to transcend the body to have a spiritual experience. Your physical senses can be a bridge to Nature and Spirit and are a wonderful way to begin your relationship with the natural world.

The Druid path honours the physical body and all aspects of the physical life on Earth. Druidry acknowledges that we live in a physical world and have physical experiences, and that matter is infused with Spirit. In the Druid cosmology, there is an energy or divinity that underlies and animates all physical matter. There is a life force energy that flows through all forms, including your physical body. This is the energy that flows through the web of life. The web of life refers to how everyone and everything is interconnected. We are one; we are all linked through this sacred connection. What affects one, affects all. In Druidry we call this life force energy *nwyfre* (Noo-eve-ray). *Nwyfre* is a Welsh word, and it refers to the pure authentic energy that flows from Divine Source or Spirit and within all creation. This energy sustains our bodies and maintains life on the planet. When you are still and quiet, when you tune into your physical body, you can sense this aliveness in your body and in the flow of life around you. Nature is empowering and can offer you a point of access to the creative and intelligent energy of the universe and to the life force energy of *nwyfre*. When you are in Nature, you are immersed in *nwyfre* and the flow of *nwyfre* within you is enhanced, offering you strength, vitality, and healing. The connection with nature via your senses and physical body helps to shift your consciousness, helping you to become present in the current moment. Being present, connected to your body and the life in Nature, helps create a sense of peace and well-being. You feel like you are a part of something bigger than yourself and that you are supported by a vast presence of unconditional love.

In Druidry, mythic tales speak to the spiritual quest: the search for transformation, enlightenment, and wisdom through Nature. These ancient wisdom tales can offer guidance and a healing energy all their own. In my Druid studies, I learned the tale of the *Well of Segais*. In this story, we hear that there is a sacred pool deep within the unseen world of Spirit, the well of wisdom. There is the seen world of everyday physical reality and there is the unseen world of Spirit. In the unseen world, we find guides and helping spirits who can offer us support and guidance on our spiritual path. In the story, the Well of Segais is surrounded by nine hazel trees. The hazel is a tree of wisdom and hazel nuts are thought to impart wisdom, knowledge, and inspiration to whoever eats them. The hazel tree drops its nuts into the water of the sacred pool.

Five streams flow into the pool. Each of the streams represents one of our five senses: sight, sound, smell, taste, and touch. The pool is the source of divine inspiration. It is said that to be truly wise, one must drink from each of the five streams and from the pool. You gain wisdom from the experiences of your physical senses and receive inspiration from the quiet stillness, the pool of awareness, that is in the centre of your being. For me, this tale suggests that experiencing the natural world through the physical senses of sight, sound, smell, taste, and touch can connect you with the source of life and with your deepest self.

Being in Nature, engaging your physical senses, helps you be embodied—connected with your body, rather than your mind. The physical senses are a bridge to presence. Being in Nature helps you quiet the unnecessary thoughts, to jump off the treadmill of continual thinking and to find the quiet peace that lives beneath your thoughts. Thinking is not important in Nature, awareness is. Awareness and presence. Presence is the portal to the deeper or higher awareness within you. When you are in this state, you are safe, and you will know when and if you need to act. It is a relaxed state, not a hypervigilant one. In this state you have greater access to your creativity and your soul's inner guidance. It can feel a bit like stepping out of the world, but it is really a stepping into the world. In this space of presence and awareness, ideas, solutions, and feelings rise in a gentle way, and are usually far more relevant than when the mind tries to ferret out a solution all on its own. The body is a doorway to your inner wisdom, and to a deeper awareness of consciousness or Spirit.

Connecting with your senses and paying attention to the sensations in your body can be a healing act. The body knows what it needs, what to eat, when to move, when to rest, and senses the world around it. The body carries the wisdom of evolution and your ancestors in its DNA and holds the knowledge of what has happened to you in your lifetime. The entire body is a sophisticated sensory system made up of billions of neurons and can receive and transmit information. Tuning in to the wisdom and intelligence of the body through your senses can help you understand how you truly feel, discover what you need, and figure out what action you need to take.

Walking is a beautiful way to engage your physical body and your senses, and to spend time in Nature. If walking is difficult for you, sit quietly in Nature (you are always free to adapt the practices in this book to your unique situation). When you are outside, it is easy to spend your time thinking about what happened yesterday, the argument you had with your co-worker, or what you are going to eat for dinner. You can be on autopilot and not notice what is going on around you. Or maybe you see the walk as a challenge, a goal to achieve. A walk in the woods can become about the destination, the number of steps you get, or your speed. Sometimes you're out with friends and having a pleasant chat but may not notice much about the world around you or how you're feeling. I invite you to see being in Nature as an opportunity to move beyond your thinking mind and connect with your body, your feelings, and the life around you.

The next time you go for a walk outside, use your physical senses and connect with Nature. Remember that you are responsible for your relationship with the natural world. Personal responsibility is one of the teachings of Nature. Always enter Nature with respect and awareness. I live in a place that is still wild—where there are bears and ticks, and there is unpredictable weather and challenging terrain. You can experience wonder and peace there, but you can also get wet, cold, or injured. It's up to you. See Appendix A for information on staying safe in the wilderness and what you need to take on a day hike in the woods. If you are going to a wilderness area or if you are not comfortable walking alone, invite a friend to come with you.

It is important to do what feels right to you. You may not be ready for a walk in the wild, but a walk in the local park or in your neighbourhood may be just what you need. You can also do this meditation on your balcony, by your window, or in your backyard. But if you can, go to a natural landscape. The potency of Nature is enhanced in places like these. Listen to your own knowing. Engage in the following practice (and all the practices in this book) with an open mind and an open heart. Over time, you'll figure out the best way for you to engage with Nature. Go into Nature as though you were going to sit or walk with a friend you haven't seen for a while, that you may have lost touch with. Consider this an opportunity to spend time and catch up with Nature—a chance to listen and to rekindle your relationship.

As you engage in the Wild Wisdom Meditation below, let go of expectations. Rather than trying to create a particular experience, be present to what you are feeling and noticing around you.

You are free to stop or change this practice at any time. Always follow your own knowing and guidance.

WILD WISDOM MEDITATION

I suggest you spend at least 30 minutes on this practice. Sometimes it can take 30 minutes to really get out of your head and your analytical mind and genuinely begin to connect to your body and the world around you, so you may want to commit an hour to this meditation.

To Begin

Take a moment and be still. Take a deep breath in and let it out slowly. Feel the Earth beneath your feet, holding and supporting you. Focus your attention on your body, starting with your feet. Notice if you feel any tension in your feet. If there is, just feel it. You don't need to do anything about it. Continue to scan all parts of the body. Move from your feet, up your legs, to your torso, chest, neck, shoulders, and face. Note any tightness or tension. When you feel ready, begin to walk in silence. Breathe in your natural rhythm.

Begin with one of the senses listed below. Take five minutes or more, focusing on each sense in turn. Remember, your senses are a bridge to experiencing the life force energy of *nwyfre* around you and within you. Experiencing Nature through your senses is a way to build relationship with the trees, plants, wind, and sky.

You may wish to carry a journal. Journaling is a spiritual practice that encourages self-reflection. At the end of the meditation, you can record observations, thoughts, and feelings that arose. You can use words, drawings, colours, pictures, or music to capture the essence of your experience. Do not go into analysis, as this will take you out of your body and into your thinking mind. Let words or images flow freely. Use colour to illustrate feelings, line for energy, and record what comes up first for you. A journal helps to ground the experience into the here and now. It can take time for the meaning of the experience to become apparent. Your journal will hold the experience for you, so you don't forget, and at a later reading, the meaning may become evident.

Sight

What do you see?

Look at the landscape around you. Notice the trees and plants, the colours of the leaves, the soil, the water, or sand. Don't try to identify plants or flowers. Just notice what you see.

Look at the space around you. Is there a quality to the light? Is the air clear or hazy? What is the sky up to? Is it cloudy, grey, or blue? Again, don't try to give names to the type of clouds or the quality of light. Just notice the things you see.

Sound

What do you hear?

First notice sounds that are far away from you. Do you hear traffic? Other people? The call of a bird?

Second, pay attention to sounds that are closer to you. Can you hear the song of birds and the rush of their wings? Can you hear the rustle of leaves? A snap of a twig? The burble of running water?

Then notice the sounds of your body, the sound of your breath moving in and out of your lungs, the sound of your heart beating.

Touch

What can you feel?

Reach out and touch Nature.

Touch a rock or pebble. How does the stone feel in your hand or against your fingertips? How does the bark of a tree feel? The petals of a flower? If there is water, touch it with your fingers, how does it feel? If possible, remove your shoes and socks and stand barefoot on the land. Does being barefoot feel different than when you have your shoes on? Sit or lie down on the ground. How does your body feel?

Smell

What can you smell?

Do you smell the rich loam of the Earth? The spicy scent of fir trees in the afternoon sun? The sweet perfume of blossoms? The earthy smell of coming rain? Can you smell a lake, stream, or the ocean? Take a moment and close your eyes and notice all the things you can smell.

Taste

What can you safely taste?

Can you taste the air? Does your food taste different when you eat it outside? Does your food taste bitter, sweeter, fresher or more alive? What about the water you drink? (Do not eat wild plants or fruit you are unfamiliar with as they may be toxic. Do not drink unfiltered or untreated water. Bring your water bottle.)

Ending the Walk

When you feel complete, stop.

Breathe in and out deeply, three times.

Give thanks to Nature and the world around you. Give thanks to your body for its ability to feel and experience the life around you.

You may wish to record your experience in your journal.

Journal Questions

What did you notice? Did your thoughts race? Did you feel more anxious or less anxious over the course of the Wild Wisdom meditation?

How does your body feel? Does it feel different than it did at the start of the meditation?

Was it easier to use one of your senses more than another?

Did anything about this experience surprise you?

If you feel called to, write down any thoughts and feelings that come up. See if you can let these thoughts rise from deep within you, rather than from deliberate analysis. You may wish to do the Wild Wisdom meditation on a regular basis. You can experiment with this meditation in different areas or landscapes, or you may wish to do it repeatedly in the same place. Returning to the same place gives you the opportunity to really get to know the landscape, to notice the changing seasons, what trees leaf out first in the spring or lose their leaves last in the fall. It gives you the chance to build a relationship with Nature, and with individual trees, plants, rocks, or water. As time goes by, you will begin to feel more in tune with the natural world.

For me, listening to the wisdom of the body, was an essential step in seeing beyond my personal story. I used to identify very strongly with my life story: my family, where I was born, what I did, my struggles and successes. I used to think that my life story was all of who I was. I spent most of my time thinking, thinking about problems, worrying about the future, analyzing, and strategizing, making up stories to explain and categorize experiences so that it all fit into my limited world view. It was exhausting and disheartening. The only place I found respite from this incessant thinking was in Nature. Nature was a haven. Nature invited me to let go of my worries and concerns. For many years, this was the greatest healing that Nature offered me. It was powerful. In time, Nature offered so much more. But this was the first step, being able to let go of thinking for a while and just feel and experience Nature through my physical senses. Your physical senses are a gateway to engage with Nature and to inhabit your own body. When you are embodied, you have access to physical and spiritual strength. You have stability and firm ground to stand on. You are connected and in relationship with the natural world around you. Being embodied fosters trust and confidence.

SACRED GIFTS

When you have had a beautiful or profound experience in Nature, you may want to take home a piece of Nature, like a rock or pinecone. It's natural to want a reminder or talisman of your time in Nature. Nature offers feelings of peace, power, and vitality, and it may offer you something more tangible, like a rock, feather, shell, or twig. These giftings are symbolic of the knowledge, understanding or experience you received from the Earth.

These are sacred gifts offered by Spirit. The rock or tree are living beings, with Spirit and consciousness. It is important to take only what is offered. Always ask permission before you take anything from Nature. Introduce yourself to the landscape, to the trees, ocean, or river and ask if they have a sacred gift for you.

Ask Nature a silent question from your heart and you will know the answer. If you feel light and expansive—that's a yes. If you feel heavy or contracted— that's a no. Try to sense which specific rock, twig, or item is your gift. Do not take the first thing you sense and take only one thing. Be respectful of Nature. Do not pick any flowers, remove any fossils, or take any living part of a tree or other plant. Offer thanks for the gift with a song, a prayer, a splash of water, or an offering of your food (only natural, biodegradable food). Offer gratitude from the depths of your heart. Ask the Spirit of the object you have taken what its gift to you is: it may be a feeling, a thought, a message, or a reminder.

You may wish to create a special box or bag made of natural materials to hold the gifts you receive from Nature. It is a place for those objects of power that have special meaning for you. Use it to collect all Nature gives you: insight and inspiration; perspective and understanding; and appreciation and knowledge of the natural world. The sacred gift box is a cauldron where Nature brews these qualities together into a deeper understanding and a richer experience of this world.

Your collection may include stones, twigs, bark, leaves, shells, pinecones, or feathers. Whatever you keep in it, the box or bag and its contents exist both in the physical world and in the unseen world of Spirit. Draw on the things in it for power or strength or to remember the lessons or feelings associated with them. As you take your personal journey though Nature, the container and its items will be a physical and an energetic or feeling record of your learnings and experiences, just as your journal is a written record. From time to time, open up your sacred gift box and look over the items you have received. Sense with your inner knowing if any of the items need to return to Nature. Let these objects go with gratitude, returning them to the place they came from, if possible.

Focusing on your senses when you are in Nature opens you to a new world. It allows you to connect with the power and wisdom of life. You notice the abundance of plants, the many shades of green, and the wild, surging joy of the natural world. Use your senses to become aware, not to interpret or analyze, or to identify plants or trees. You are in Nature not to intellectualize it but to be in communion with it. When you tune into your body and senses, you open the door to a deeper connection with the life around you and within you. With time, you will merge with the landscape around you.

Chapter Two: Inner Wisdom

Nature is a place where you can be yourself. There is no role to play or mask to wear. It is a tremendous relief to be able to show up just as you are. Nature has no agenda and makes no judgments. And so, when you are immersed in the simplicity and beauty of Nature, you stop judging yourself. You can drop your masks and the beliefs you hold about yourself, and let Nature help you feel into the truth of who you are.

In this chapter, you will discover Nature as a path to this inner wisdom. When you go to Nature without expectations, something special happens. You feel better, lighter, more peaceful. You come to understand that you are part of something bigger than yourself. If you just look, Nature reveals the many connections in the web of life. You see the sun feeding plants, the plants feeding deer, and the deer feeding the wolves. You notice the complex web of support, of giving and receiving, that sustains life in Nature—soil and water, sun and air, plants and animals, and you. For you, too, are a part of this complex web. You begin to see how the web of life exists beyond the physical world and encompasses the mental, emotional, and spiritual aspects of your being. You begin to understand the power of your thoughts and feelings. You begin to have more respect for all beings, including yourself. Over time, you may find that Nature changes how you feel and how you move through the world. When you build relationship with the natural world, you create a natural harmony and balance within you.

Your inner self's natural state is one of joy and peace, but you can lose that joy and peace as you become lost in the busyness of daily living. Life can become a never-ending treadmill—a series of tasks to complete and goals to accomplish. When you do achieve your goals, the satisfaction may be fleeting as you immediately turn toward the next target. You may feel empty, and that life is pointless.

Nature can give you a fresh perspective. In the quiet of Nature, everything that seems so crucial and worrisome in your day-to-day life falls away and tranquility descends. You come away from time spent in Nature calm, peaceful, happy, and energized. There is a depth to you that cannot be measured by your financial success or your accomplishments. You are so much more than any of these. You are more than your thoughts and emotions. You are more than who you think you are, and more than what you do. You are more than the responsibilities you carry. Nature helps you to find your deeper self, your soul self, and connects you to your inner knowing and intuition. Your inner knowing lives within you. It is the intuition that looks out for you and holds you in compassion. Your inner knowing, your soul self, is an expression of Divine Source energy. Source is expressed through you. When you connect with your inner knowing, you connect with the greater life. You connect with the Spirit that lives and moves through everything. There is joy, abundance, and support that lives within and around you. When you connect with your intuition and your calm center, you can weather life's storms better. You may find you can accomplish more with less effort. Life is more relaxed when the challenging times come, and you have a support system in place to help you get through them. You can access your inner knowing to guide you through life's difficulties. If you are having negative thoughts or feeling low, you can recall the peace and quiet you feel in the natural world. Nature can shift your thoughts and feelings to more positive ones.

When you connect with your inner knowing, creativity, joy, inspiration, and peace allow you to transcend all the beliefs, stories, and judgments you may hold. Nature will help you see that you are not broken, but whole, that you are not alone, but part of life. When you access your inner wisdom, you will find answers to the important questions you may have about your life. What is your purpose? How do you fit in?

When you are in relationship with Nature, there is a feeling of quiet, and trust. I used to think that this quiet space within was a place of utter stillness, but it's not. There is a flow and ease available to you in this state that I call a grounded flow. From this place, there is no need to rush or panic. You can meet the challenges in your life with less stress and drama. The surface of the water may be choppy, but beneath the waves, it is calm.

GROUNDED FLOW PRACTICE

During my studies with The Order of Bards, Ovates, and Druids, I learned how to become aware of the energy of the Earth and Sky. As I studied more, I learned how to move from awareness of the energy to communion with it. The Grounded Flow practice evolved from these teachings. I offer this practice to help you feel strong and grounded on the Earth, to find the quiet centre within you, and to feel the flow of life move through you.

If possible, go out to a natural or wild place. If you can't do this, don't worry. This practice can be done anywhere, even indoors, any time you want (or need) to experience grounded flow. It's also a perfect practice to start your day.

Sit or stand with your feet firmly on the ground. Begin with your breath. Take three deep breaths, in through your nose and out through your mouth. Settle into your body. Now, imagine you are a tree, deeply rooted in the Earth. Visualize the green light of the Earth moving up your roots from the dark, rich soil. Feel your trunk, sturdy and strong, supporting you. Feel your branches reaching to the sky. Sense the golden light of the sun entering your leaves and flowing back down your trunk to your roots. Sense the gold and green lights as they move through your body, clearing, healing, and revitalizing you before they form a protective circle of light around you. You are immersed in light, safe and rooted to the Earth.

At first, when you do this practice, you may feel bored, or stupid, or irritated. If this happens, gently bring your focus back to the feeling of being a tree. Follow the path of your breath as it moves in and out of your body. Imagine breathing in peace and strength and breathing out stress and worry. Imagine the flow of light moving through you, supporting, nurturing, and protecting you.

When you feel complete, release the circle of light and come back to the here and now.

Journal Questions

Did you notice the life force energy flowing through you? Describe what it felt like or which parts of your body were most sensitive to it.

How did you feel after practicing Grounded Flow? Did you have any flashes of insight?

When and how might you bring this feeling or practice into your life?

If you did not feel any light flowing through you, don't despair! It can take time to feel the energy around you. Go back to your physical body. Focus on the sensation of the Earth beneath you and the air on your skin. Use your five senses to connect with the life force energy in your body. Focus on your breath. Following the path of your breath is an ancient practice that helps you connect with your calm centre. Keep practicing. Be patient. Just allow what is true for you in the present moment without judgement or expectation. It's all right to use your imagination too. Imagination is not illusion, it is sacred.

There was a time when my family was experiencing financial stress. I offer the experience below to illustrate how Nature can lift you up and restore tranquility, even when you are in distress.

Journal Entry: A Winter's Day

I am beyond anxious, teetering on the edge of hysteria. My mind is looping and racing over the same negative thoughts repeatedly. I feel helpless. I find myself driving out to the wilderness; the woods beckon to me. Snow crunches under my feet as I start up the main trail. I decide to take a path I've never walked before. Soon I find myself on a narrow trail that threads its way through the aspens. It is well-trod, no snowshoes required, and I am alone on the trail today. The slender trees surround me as I walk, gathering me in.

I labour up and down the hills as the path takes me deeper into the woods. I'm breathing heavily, and I feel like I'm trying to outrun my thoughts, trying to leave my emotions and fear behind. At last, I stop, out of breath. This will not do.

I plunge off the path into the deep snow and approach a fir tree. I ask if I may spend some time with it. I hear a yes. It is tall, and I place my hand on its rough bark. Immediately I feel soothed. My heart quiets as I rest my forehead on the weathered trunk. Closing my eyes, I feel the tree supporting me. I become aware of the incredible peace of the woodland. In winter, the silence is profound. There is a depth of quiet stillness that permeates my whirlwind of feelings. My thoughts slow to a stop, and I come to rest in the embrace of this tree. I feel the land around me begin to spin, the tree and I are on solid ground, the still point of the centre, bound together as the world around us turns and expands. Everything lives in this space, all possibility, opportunity, creativity, beauty, death, and life. I stay awhile, and then I thank the tree. I resume my walk, but now I am peaceful. I feel like the life of the greenwood lives in me, and all the worries I brought with me have disappeared. I sing as I walk. I am joyful and full of gratitude.

FINDING SELF LOVE AND YOUR INNER VOICE

Nature soothes your pain and loves you just as you are. Nature shows you how to love yourself. This is a great gift of Nature, a powerful healing. For much of my life, I looked outside of myself for love and approval. I measured myself by others' perceptions and accepted their beliefs, both individual and cultural, as my own. The trouble was, I didn't fit into this world very well. I felt like an outsider. Well-meaning people tried to help me by sharing their experiences and what worked for them. Unfortunately, I would take everything they said as a directive. I did not weigh their advice with my own knowing, my own truth. I blindly accepted their beliefs—what was true for them—as my own. I also accepted their negative judgments and projections. I thought that I wasn't worth very much, that I had no skills and wasn't good for anything. I was miserable. I'm embarrassed to say how long I looked outside myself for validation, how long it took for me to hear my own truth and inner voice. I didn't trust my knowing. I didn't trust that life had my back. I thought I had to control and manipulate situations and people to get my needs met. Even now, it's not always clear to me whose voice I'm hearing in my head. Is it my inner critic? My mother or father? My boss? There are times when doubt, fear, and worry can crowd out your inner knowing. When you spend time in Nature, it's easier to hear the truth of your being. Nature creates a calm space for you to listen to your soul's truth.

I used to think that love meant giving up every part of yourself and every resource you had to support others. I thought love was pain, loss, and sacrifice. I thought it was selfish, and the opposite of spirituality, to put yourself first. Nature helped me to see and feel differently. Trees stand tall. They do not judge. They know they are a vital part of the ecosystem they live in. They contribute to the world around them just by being who they are. It is the same for people. You must have love, compassion, and respect for yourself before you can offer them to others. The trees show you how to stand strong in yourself. They teach you that your unique offering to the world isn't what you do, but who you are. The trees are held in the divine love of all that is, and so are you. This is the magic of Nature. When you open your eyes and listen deeply, you can hear Nature's teachings. They were always there. They are part of you. Nature is the path back home to your own truth and your own voice.

Nature is the cauldron for healing and transformation. Nature accepts and loves you just as you are, so you can love yourself. Nature doesn't see you as a victim or as broken, but whole and well, so you can see yourself that way too. Nature is your witness and will hold a safe space for you. Love, acceptance, strength, vitality, peace, and joy, all that Nature offers, lead you to wholeness and toward hearing and trusting your inner voice.

At first, the only time I could hear my inner voice and find my calm centre was when I was physically in Nature. Over time, it felt like Nature lived in me. Most of us feel stress, pressure, or anxiety. Fear usually comes from worrying about something that has not happened yet—getting sick, running out of money, losing your job. We rarely take a break from all this thinking and worry, and so we live in a state of perpetual anxiety.

There are hidden paths to our inner knowing, tracks in the snow that we can miss in our anxious state. Nature helps you find these hidden trails by opening the door to a different feeling and a different experience. Nature heals, teaches, guides, and comforts. Nature knows how to restore herself. Because you are part of Nature, you can restore yourself, too. When you pay attention, Nature shows you how to live. She guides you back to the truth of your being, to the inner wisdom and intuition of the soul self that lives within you and connects you to something greater than yourself.

CULTIVATING GRATITUDE

Every moment is different. Your thinking mind likes to analyze and create predetermined responses. It wants to know the correct answer ahead of time, assuming that every situation is the same as it has experienced before. This pattern can leave you trapped in a loop, neither changing nor growing. Grounded Flow invites you to be fully present and to notice the energy and the feeling you are experiencing right now. This level of presence is your natural state. When you are aware and present, you can respond to the truth of this moment. Practice Grounded Flow—be quiet, observe, and listen. The appropriate response will arise from within. The response may be an action, or it may be a new feeling or a new way of looking at something. The Grounded Flow practice will help you access your intuition and awaken you to the beauty in Nature.

Noticing the beauty around you expands your perspective and connects you to life. Beauty, in Nature, in art, in any form, inspires and uplifts you. Experiencing beauty offers you a new feeling and fresh insight. It fosters gratitude and appreciation. The beauty you encounter in Nature and the gratitude it inspires connect you to your deeper Self and Spirit. Practicing gratitude and appreciation can transform your life and help you feel lighter, joyful, and more peaceful. If you need to enhance your ability to feel gratitude and appreciation, try the following practice in appreciating the beauty of Nature.

GROUNDED FLOW PRACTICE: APPRECIATING BEAUTY

Start the Grounded Flow practice. When you feel calm and aware of the flow of light and energy surrounding and protecting you, begin to pay attention to the beauty that is all around you. The more you see the beauty and the wild abundance of life around you, the more beauty begins to fill up every aspect of your life. Appreciate the many gifts and blessings that Nature showers on you every moment of every day. Feeling grateful for the wonder and beauty of Nature helps you feel more positive and experience a general sense of well-being. This practice can be done sitting in Nature or walking.

When you are ready, release the circle of light and give a silent thanks to the place you visited. Give thanks to your body and being for the experience. You may also want to leave a natural offering, like birdseed or a splash of water, to say thank you to Nature. Sense the space around you and see if Nature has a gift for your sacred gift box. It should be something that calls to you, like a small stone to remind you of the Earth and the experience of feeling grounded, or a leaf that has fallen from the tree, carried by the wind, to remind you of the feeling of flow.

Journal Questions

What did you appreciate most from this experience? What are you grateful for?

How did this practice make you feel?

How can you incorporate into your daily life the practice of noticing the beauty around you?

Nature is your mirror. All the beauty, abundance, energy, vitality, and peace that you see and experience in Nature lives within you too. As you spend time in the natural world and feel the presence and strength of the flora and fauna flow into you, you become aware of your own presence and power. You breathe in the fresh air, and it flows into every cell, balancing, clearing, and energizing you. You feel the warmth of the sun on your face and are reminded that the sun supports you and all life on the planet, without expectation. You can practice Grounded Flow anytime. From this place you can connect to the life around you and continue to build your relationship with the natural world.

ACCESSING EMOTIONS AND INSIGHTS

As you commune with Nature and connect to your inner wisdom, you may feel unexpected emotions, like a sea of rage or a great sorrow. You may feel shame and fear, too. This connection with Nature and your soul self is an invitation to live authentically, to acknowledge and be aware of everything that is true for you. It will shine a light on what needs healing in your life.

There may be trauma you have buried deep inside you, something about yourself you dislike and disown, some emotion that weighs you down. Shamanic teachings indicate that many different experiences may be felt as trauma. Abuse can be traumatic, of course, but it's not the only kind of trauma. A child might experience the first day of school or falling out of a tree as traumatic. Unresolved issues can lead to anxiety, depression, or illness and can keep us stuck, leaving us unable to access our own strength and impairing our ability to receive. Nature creates a safe space for feelings related to trauma to surface. There is nothing you really need to do but feel them and accept them with no judgment. Do not think about or analyze them, just know you are safe and breathe through the experience. Nature will help calm your anxiety and fear.

I was surprised when I first discovered the rage within me. I was always 'nice' to everyone. I always tried to do the right thing and to meet everybody else's needs. I had no idea I was full of rage. I had judged anger to be unacceptable and buried it deep within me, so I could pretend it wasn't there. Many of us are taught that feeling anger is not okay. I have since come to understand that all of our emotions are guideposts. They point a direction for you, and provide information about beliefs that need your attention, a personal boundary that may have been violated, and can be part of the healing process. A belief is a story or an explanation you have created to make sense of, or give meaning to, the world around you and how you fit into that world. A belief can feel very real, but that doesn't mean it's true. I came to understand that my feelings of rage stemmed from a belief that I was not enough, not valued, not seen by the people in my life. Feelings of fear arose from a belief that life did not have my back, that I was at the mercy of the world. Nature opened a door to a deeper understanding. Nature helped me connect to my inner wisdom. It was a safe space to feel everything I had to feel. The deep love I felt from Nature, that I received from Divine Spirit, created a space to sit with these feelings and thoughts. I knew I was loved and safe; I was not bad or broken. Time spent in Nature allowed me to access and accept my shadow parts and see my light. Nature helped me to accept myself and discover who I truly am. I learned to be present with what is and to hear my inner wisdom. In this state, I could joyfully share the real me with others. This sharing gave me, and still gives me, wholeness, balance, peace, and purpose. Nature is a source of creativity and inspiration and enables you to live from your heart and truth.

Many of us have been taught to fear both Nature and our instinctive inner self. We have been told they are wild, unpredictable, and untamed and should be avoided, rather than accepted, appreciated, and honoured. You may have received the message that Nature is not to be trusted, that it's out to get you. Nature is not out to get you. It has no judgment. It just is. You may experience fear in Nature because the natural world is beyond your control. You may feel vulnerable in the face of its power and in the face of your inner strength and power.

Nature can mirror back to you what you're feeling. If you feel fear in Nature, start where you feel safe, like your backyard or a local park. When you feel ready, go out into a wilder space with a friend. You don't have to go far. Remember that the power and strength you feel in Nature, the power you fear, also lives within you. It is part of you. Take your time and ask Spirit for help. Listen to your intuition. You know when things don't feel right. Listen to your inner guidance. Ask it for what you need to feel safe and to open your heart to a relationship with Nature. It will let you know when you are ready to go into Nature, how long to stay, and which path to take.

Journal Questions

What powerful emotions have been arising for you during your time in nature?

What glimmers of inner knowing and intuition have you experienced?

Did Nature inspire you in some way?

What if you could trust in life, trust in the Divine? How might your life change if you embraced the unknown?

UNCOVERING INNER GUIDANCE AND DIRECTION

I believe that Nature will lead you to your deeper self and a wider understanding of who you are and why you're here. Many of us identify who we are with our body, our thoughts, our emotions, where we live, or our job. We tend to experience life from our thinking mind and can get caught up in the swirl of emotions, thoughts, and beliefs, rather than living from the place of our inner self, the conscious awareness that is the soul self or the higher or deepest self. This is the source of our intuition and inner wisdom. You are not your body, your thoughts, or your emotions. You are the conscious awareness that experiences life through the senses of the body, the thoughts of the mind, and the feelings of the heart. Sometimes we get distracted by everything we are experiencing in the world. We can lose touch with our inner self, with our inner wisdom. When we engage our inner wisdom, a deep, quiet truth emerges. We don't have to have knee-jerk reactions based upon our past experiences or our beliefs. We can respond from awareness. There is an awareness that flows from Nature and the sacred. Our thoughts are often filtered through our experiences, stories, and beliefs. When thoughts flow instead through awareness, from the still quiet place within us, they can reflect our truth.

Each of us receives intuitive guidance differently. Some people are clairvoyant—they see images. Others are clairaudient—they hear messages as a voice in their head. Some people feel sensations in their body, or smell information. Others receive information and inspiration as a deep knowing. Each of us can develop all these ways of receiving. Through experience, you will discover how you best receive intuitive guidance.

If I'm grappling with a problem or an emotion, I go to Nature and release it into the wild, I release it to Spirit. As I walk or spend time in Nature, out on the trail or with the tree in my backyard, I often write in my journal. I invite you to do the same. This practice is about connecting to your inner wisdom to receive higher guidance:

Journal Questions

What do you need right now?

What do you long to create in your life?

What do you need to change or do differently?

If you don't know the answers, that's okay too. Just offer the situation to Spirit and let it go. All you need to do is be present and listen over the coming days and the ideas, feelings, thoughts, and knowing, will arise from the well of your being. It's good to ask for help with everyday things as well as with big questions. The path will unfold for you one step at a time.

We are all responsible for our own health and well-being. Only you carry the answers for you. However, please know that you are always supported. There is support from Spirit, from Nature, and from other people. You don't have to figure things out all by yourself. There may be times when you need to work with a therapist, medical doctor, or other helping professional who can support your healing. If you feel overwhelmed, seek professional help.

It can be hard to know if the voice you hear is the truth of your inner self or if it flows from your thinking mind, from a belief or judgment you hold. It can be hard to know if you are making things up or if they're real. Remember this: Your inner or soul self will never judge you, or be negative, or tell you to hurt yourself or another. Your inner self is full of unconditional love and is a positive force. If you hear negative thoughts, it is not truth speaking. If you hear judgement, it is not truth speaking. Your inner guidance and your helping spirits will never ask you to go against your values or make you feel bad about yourself. If you feel mired in negativity, I recommend you seek professional help to support you.

When I first began this relationship with my inner self and with Nature, I wasn't sure if it was real or if I was making it up. One way I learned to trust the wisdom I received was to accept that imagination was a gift of the soul, and that when I worked within the circle of light of the Grounded Flow practice, I could trust the outcome. This circle of light is a circle of protection of divine light and love. I kept my thoughts focused on this light, this loving presence I knew I could trust. It became easier with practice.

I believe the wisdom you seek lives within you, and Nature can help you access this guidance. Nature can help take you beyond your personal story and beliefs and guide your soul into deeper communion with Divine Spirit. Listening to your inner wisdom helps you understand your own struggles, find recurring patterns in your life, and know what your next steps could be. Your inner wisdom helps you understand what your soul is here to learn in this life and what you are here to share. Your inner wisdom shows you how to live your truth. It shows you what brings you joy, and what you really want. From this place of deep connection, you can share your contribution with the world.

Chapter Three: Tree Wisdom

I LOVE TREES. I LOVE the woods. I feel most myself when surrounded by trees. You may prefer the ocean or the desert—all of Nature can offer you a path home to yourself. You can be in relationship with any aspect of Nature. I will take you on a journey through the forest, but you can apply the teachings of the trees to all of Nature. I wish to awaken you to the ancient wisdom that lives in the Earth. There is clarity, aliveness, and joy that bubbles up from the well of your being when you are in Nature. If you are still and quiet, you will discover the inner landscape of your soul.

Trees have offered humanity so many things: beauty, food, wood for shelter and fuel, and healing medicine. They filter our air and provide shelter and food for birds and plants. Trees sequester carbon, give off water and oxygen, and help to moderate the climate. I'm sure we have all appreciated the shade of a tree on a hot day. Trees are often used as markers in the physical landscape and help us navigate our world. They are essential symbols for many cultures and play a vital role in many myths and religions. The Tree of Life connects all realms, holds wisdom, and is a symbol of connection, eternity, and harmony.

Trees carry threefold wisdom through their roots, trunk, and branches. Their roots anchor them to the Earth, to the here and now, and suggest strength and endurance. The roots offer stability, carry nutrients and water up from the Earth, and create a web of connections beneath the surface that hold memory and communicate with other trees. The trunk connects Earth to the heavens, allowing life from the Earth to move up the tree and carry the sun's energy to the roots. The trunk is a two-lane highway that connects Earth and Sky, just as we are connectors of the energy of the Earth and Sky. The branches and canopy are symbolic of growth, abundance, and the cosmos. The interlacing canopy receives energy from the sun through photosynthesis, bringing the sun's power to Earth. Many trees drop their leaves in the fall and are reborn in the spring. This speaks to us of the never-ending cycle of birth, death, and re-birth. Trees give voice to the changing seasons and rhythms in our own lives and offer shelter, nurturing, sustenance, and hope for our bodies and spirits. Trees stand and accept what comes their way—good and bad, sunshine and rain, storms and breezes, disease and insects. They live with their wounds without judgment and create anew from a place of acceptance.

It's no wonder that people have had a special relationship with trees over the centuries. As a Druid, I am particularly fond of trees. When you talk to a tree, the tree listens. When you listen to a tree, the tree offers you a gift in return. Trees tell you the truth. The lessons of the forest are here and now. Each tree is like a person, a unique being with its own strengths and attributes. Trees provide their own healing energy. I believe each tree has its own voice and its own song, and carries vitality, wisdom, and knowledge. Trees are linked to the web of life, as you are, and can share their wisdom with you. We are all in relationship with one another. When we attune to or feel the life force energy or *nwyfre* that lives in all things, animate and inanimate, seen and unseen, we sense our place within the world and understand the state of our relationship. You can connect with the spirit of a tree, and the tree will offer its teachings and the energy it carries.

As you may recall from the beginning of the book, it was a tree that woke me up so many years ago. That Western red cedar set me on the path of Shamanism and Druidry and was indeed the gateway to a new life for me. I'm so grateful to that tree, and when I drop into my body, when I am quiet and listen, I can find the feeling of that tree within me. I can connect with that tree through time and space. I received the blessings of the tree and the woods that day. I invite you, too, to open yourself to a relationship with these calm, peaceful, and wise beings.

Trees offer us perspective and are thought by many to carry knowledge of their time on Earth. Trees are long-lived beings—many live for over 500 years.

The trees around you were likely here before you were born and will be living long after your death. They tend to have quiet, slow energy. It may take time for you to slow down enough to connect with them. Be patient. With practice you will learn to commune with the spirit in trees and in all things. You will cease being the observer and become one with or a part of whatever you are observing. When you become one with a tree, you truly begin to know it. To do this, you must recognize the spirit of the tree, and the intelligence of its being. You must understand that trees are not soulless, stupid, or inert. When you come to this understanding, you expand your world. You acknowledge the reality of your relationship to all beings.

TALKING TO TREES

By now, you may be wondering: "Can I talk to a tree?"

The answer is yes! Now, I understand that you may feel ridiculous "talking" to a tree. I invite you to let go of any judgment or expectation. Enter the experience with an open mind and an open heart.

Start by taking a walk in a natural area. A great way to begin a dialogue with a tree is simply to pay attention. Notice the different trees you encounter. Notice how they look and how they feel. Do they feel different from each other? Do they feel old, young, happy, wise, cheeky, indifferent?

Then notice how the trees make you feel. Do you feel curious, excited, intimidated, interested? Your connection with the trees may be soft and fleeting, like a butterfly's wings, just brushing the edge of your awareness. It may come like a lightning bolt of energy. Or you may feel nothing at all. There is no wrong way. Think of it as meeting someone for the very first time; you may not hug, but you do shake hands. Over time, the relationship grows, and you share more, and trust more. It's the same with trees.

Take a walk like this several times. It is ideal if you can take the same route, passing the same trees repeatedly. This will help you to begin a relationship with these trees. When you feel comfortable, send them a silent greeting as you go by.

Once you're comfortable with this practice, notice if there is a particular tree you feel drawn to. (If you are not able to go directly to a tree, find a photo of a tree.) Don't worry if you don't know what kind of tree it is. It is more important to meet the tree as a being, to know its feeling rather than its scientific or common name. In time, you may learn the type of tree it is, and it may share its name with you. Slow down and stop before the tree. Introduce yourself and ask if you can sit with it awhile. Explain that you wish to connect with and speak to it. If you sense a yes, approach the tree with respect. If you feel a no, go ask another tree.

Once you have found a tree, turn your attention to your breath. Breath connects us to all that is. Following the path of your breath brings you into your body and anchors you in the moment. Engage in the Grounded Flow exercise. Take three deep breaths. Imagine the green light of the Earth and the golden light of the Sky flowing through you, clearing, healing, and forming a protective circle of light around you and the tree. When you feel calm and present, continue. Touch the tree with your hand. Feel the bark. Connect with the tree; let a welcome flow to it through your hand. Feel the life in the tree. Lean or sit against the tree. Feel it supporting you, its strength anchoring you to the Earth.

To commune with a tree, you need to go deeper than thought. Let go of thinking and just be aware of the tree. Shift from your everyday world to your inner world, your inner landscape.

Feel the profound presence that lives within the tree. You may wish to imagine seeing through the eyes of the spirit of the tree. How does the world look and feel from this perspective?

If you wish, ask the tree if it has a message for you. Ask it to show you what its gifts are. Pay attention to any thoughts, feelings, or impressions that arise. Don't get lost in your thoughts, worries, or complaints. If you do, stop. Breathe. Feel the life in your body, then connect with the tree again. Be quiet, listen and feel. You may wish to record your thoughts and feelings in your journal as you sit with the tree.

When you feel complete, release the circle of protective light that surrounds you and ask for blessings upon the tree.

Journal Questions

What did it feel like to spend time with the tree?

Did you feel a flow of energy from the tree strengthening or inspiring you?

What was it like to see through the eyes of the tree?

Did you receive a message or a feeling from the tree? If so, record the
tree's message.

What does the tree show you about how to live and be in this world?

After you have practiced connecting with the spirit of trees, find a special
natural place that you can visit again and again. Spend as much time there as
you can. Become familiar with the trees that live there. Notice the changing
seasons. Pay attention to which trees leaf out first in the spring, to the quality
of the light, and to the sky beyond the trees. Immerse yourself in Nature and
listen. Breathe and listen.

Notice how the trees feel. Does this feeling change with each day, or with
the different seasons? Can you feel the flow of *nwyfre* in the trees, between the
trees, within yourself? Do you come away inspired to embark on a new project
or with an answer to a problem that's been eluding you? Notice what changes
for you as you continue to spend time in the woods or in meditation with your
tree friends.

Every part of the tree carries its spirit. If there is a cone, leaf, or branch on the
ground, ask the tree if you may take it with you for your sacred gift box. If you
feel a yes, take it as a reminder of your meeting and a way to connect with the
energy and spirit of the tree when you are at home. Remember not to take the
first thing you see, and to take only one thing. Don't cut or pull anything off a
living tree. Even if the tree is dead, it's essential to ask permission first. The spirit
of the tree lives in the deadwood too.

Remember to be respectful. Offer thanks to the tree for the sacred gift and
for the gift of the time it gave you. Ask it if there is something it requires from
you, a gift you can offer it in return. I believe we receive as we give. Your gift to
the tree may be water, seed, song, or prayer. (Please be sure to leave only biodegradable items). It may be supporting a reforestation project or planting a tree
in your yard. Listen and you will know what you can give.

The tree you connect with may become a special friend to you. You may
wish to return to it many times. Or you may want to meet a variety of trees.
Listen to what your inner guidance tells you and you will know the best path
forward for you.

JOURNAL ENTRY: DANCES WITH TREES

I stand in the forest. Slender trunks crowd around me, pale white in the dimness of the grey afternoon. I step close to one tall tree and clasp my hand around the trunk. The touch is electric. Strength and grace flow from the bark to my hand.

I press my whole body against the tree, heart to heartwood. My eyes are drawn up to the treetops. The gold leaves of autumn gleam dully, wet with rain. Above me, clouds run with the wind. The top of the tree moves in a slow waltz. I feel as though I'm turning, even though my feet are not moving. It is my soul that dances with the trees, dances with the wind. The trees whisper to each other, trembling and shaking, as aspen do. The canopy is alive with movement, yet on the ground, all is still.

My heart beats in rhythm with the tree, in rhythm with the Earth. The tree fills me with strength and peace. Our spirits mesh. I am in the tree, and the tree is in me. There is no separation. We Are One.

It is hard to explain. Words fall short. One must experience firsthand that leaping into the rush of spirit, dancing with creation in the arms of a tree.

Enter the wild wood and walk amongst the trees. Take a moment to stand with a tree, invite it to dance with you. Listen deeply and feel its quiet wisdom and grace. Dance with the trees and feel truth and beauty opening within you.

I have been fortunate to work with many different trees. I recall sitting among some fir trees in a city park. I was grappling with a big decision about my future career. It was a significant fork in the road for me. One choice would take me down the path of veterinary medicine and the other would take me toward becoming a biologist. I didn't know what to do. Just sitting in the quiet presence of a cluster of fir trees soothed me and helped me to find the source of my inner guidance. After my time with the trees, I knew what I had to do, even though it was a difficult choice. I have never regretted my decision. I know that the trees helped me to access my inner wisdom, to make a choice aligned with my soul's path and truth.

One of the first trees I worked with was a willow in my backyard. I had no idea if I could work with a tree or talk with one—this was long before I started my studies, and shortly after my wakeup call from the red cedar. But I had heard that trees could carry prayers and messages to loved ones who had passed away, and it was late on Hallowe'en, also known as Samhain, when the veil between the worlds is thinner. And so, I ventured out to the unkempt corner of the yard, full of spiders and mystery, where the willow lives. In one hand I held a candle, in the other a shot of whisky. The sky was black, with no light from the moon or stars.

When I got to the willow, I toasted my lost loved ones and poured the whisky down the tree's trunk. I asked the tree to take my prayers to my loved ones. The moment I asked, a sudden breeze came and rustled the dry leaves that still clung to the willow's branches. It was a response from Spirit, and I must confess it scared me! I gave my thanks and hurried back inside to the warmth and light of my home. I had not expected anything to happen. I thought I was a bit crazy to be out there offering whisky to a tree, but I asked the willow to carry my prayers, and I received an answer. I have done this ritual of honour to my ancestors every Samhain since.

I go to that willow often. I also make prayer ribbons (of natural biodegradable materials) to hang on various trees in my yard, to carry messages and prayers of supplication and gratitude to Spirit for the people, animals, and lands I love. Trees, as connectors of Earth and Sky, are well suited to carry our prayers. In Celtic lands, people tie bits of cloth to trees around sacred wells as a form of prayer and supplication. These trees are known as clootie trees.

FOREST SINGING

I often go and sit with trees in a nearby wilderness area. These are special times. I sit, observe, and feel. I immerse myself in Nature and soak up the peace and quiet of the woods. Sometimes I sing. I love to sing to the trees, to the Earth, to Spirit. Singing is an offering of love and connection. We are all part of the Song of Life. Each of us is an emanation of Source or Divine Spirit; each of us has our own vibration, or energy, our own note to sing in the Song of Life. In Druidry, a Bard is someone who knows the creative power of sound, of their own voice. There is power, magic, and beauty in the sound of your voice. I will sit in the woods and hum, just hum, what feels like the right note to sound. Sometimes I sing songs or chants that I know and sometimes I just sing vowel sounds, like "ah" or "oo." Whenever I do this, I feel a response from the natural world.

Once I was out horseback riding with my friends. We stopped for lunch in a grassy meadow high on a ridge that looked out over the valley below. The mountains were so close I felt I could touch them. I stood beside my horse, and I started to sing. It was a song of love and gratitude—an offering to Nature. I could feel the Earth respond with a bubbling of energy that rose from the ground and into my feet, a flow of wisdom beyond my understanding. I could feel a presence, like the Nature spirits were all listening. I turned around to discover I had an audience of four horses, all listening attentively! Singing is a beautiful way to build relationship with the natural world and with animals!

Another time we were riding, I sang as we went. A bird appeared and followed us for an exceptionally long time. To me, this is evidence of another bridge that was built between myself, my horse, the land, and the bird. Your voice is a powerful creator and connector. As you sound your note in the song of life, the web responds. We are all connected. It's like you ring a bell and the door opens.

Singing creates a bond between you and the Earth. You can feel the power rise with the song, even when your voice sounds weak. Once I sang a song of gratitude to the ocean. I felt self-conscious and sang very quietly. I did not feel very powerful that day, and yet, I could sense the ocean receiving my gift and I left feeling more empowered. Another time, as I stood and sang to the Earth and the trees, a family of ravens came and sat in the tree above me, followed by small songbirds. A bird I didn't know showed up too. I believe they could sense the love and gratitude in the song, and they responded.

I have a frame drum. When I hold it to my mouth, I can sing along the surface of the drum. My breath flows across the drum, and I can find the note that resonates with the drum. The drum has a note and a voice too. When you match the drum's voice with your note, the drum sings. Once I stood at the fence of the paddock. My horse, Smoke, was on the other side. I started to play the drum, but the energy was too strong, and he became overly excited. I decided to sing into the drum, to sound the drum's note, and the drum rang with the sound. Smoke approached and put his mouth against the drum too. He was trying to sing into the drum. It was a beautiful moment of connection between myself, Smoke, the drum, and Spirit.

I sing from a place of love and gratitude, and I receive love and gratitude in return. You might want to practice sounding a note, when you are in the shower, maybe, and when you are outside. You may also want to sit with a tree and see if you can hear its song or sound. If you do, sing that note back to the tree. When you sing to the tree, does the tree respond in any way? Can you feel its energy? Nature loves music, especially your voice. It is a beautiful way to connect with your soul self and build a bridge of loving connection with the natural world.

Try it and see what happens. Your singing doesn't have to sound pretty. It doesn't have to sound like anything. We can all hum or sound an "oo" or an "ah." It is the love and intention you put into the sound that matters, not the sound itself. Singing is an offering of your voice, your note, that connects you with Spirit within you and within the web of life. In communion, you become everything, and everything becomes you. You become one with all that is.

As you can tell, I love the forest. It is the place where I feel most myself. I always find a gift or blessing there. Sometimes it is peace, or perspective, or a wild surge of power from a summer storm. It might be the bright red of a rosehip or a splash of white from dainty flowers on the ground. The woods always lead me back home to my inner self, to my truth and to the greater life of Spirit. A forest is a special place. No tree stands alone, each is supported by the other trees, in community. All aspects of the woodland are interconnected—the soil, the water, the sunlight, the animals. Our life is like that too. We don't stand alone but are immersed in and connected to a vast community of beings and energies that love and support us. I would invite you, in your daily life, to pay attention to the many gifts you have received from trees. The life of a tree was given for your paper, tables, chairs, and home. Respect and honour this gifting of life and ask yourself how you can support the trees in return.

TREE SPIRIT GUIDE MEDITATION

I invite you on a visualization meditation to meet a tree spirit guide. The tree you visualize might be a tree you know well in the physical world, or it might be a tree that you imagine. This tree holds great wisdom and love. This will be the tree that you can visit anytime in your inner world, to rest, to listen, to be in

Nature, to be held, and to receive guidance and wisdom. Take a moment to read through the visualization first so you become familiar with it.

To begin, find a quiet place to sit or lie down where you will not be disturbed. Take three deep breaths. Complete the Grounded Flow practice, creating a luminous circle of protective energy around you. When you are ready, imagine yourself on the edge of a vast forest. There is a smooth path before your feet, and you decide to follow it deeper into the woods. As you walk, you notice the time of day, the colours around you, and how the trees smell. You hear the birds, the wind in the trees, and your own footfalls. Your breath is calm and smooth, breathing in and breathing out. You notice that this is a place like no other. Every kind of tree in the world lives here, including some you don't recognize. It is a beautiful place. You feel safe and protected.

You follow the path as it begins to climb up a hill. The path winds round and round the hill and eventually you emerge above the tree line. The top of the hill is hidden by rocky crags and mist. At last, you reach the top. The mist clears and you see a single tree. This is your tree spirit guide. Take time to notice the overall shape of the tree. Is it slender and tall? Is it wide and gnarly? You feel the tree beckoning to you, and you approach it. As you do, imagine placing your heart—the love you feel—into your hands, then reach out and touch the tree with your palm. Imagine the love from your heart flowing toward the heart of the tree. As you touch the tree, notice if its bark is smooth or rough.

Look up and notice the patterns of the branches above you. Pay attention to whether the tree has needles or leaves. Whichever it has, reach out and touch them. Are they waxy? Smooth? Spiky? What shape are they? Notice the smell of the tree, whether it is spicy or sweet. See if there are any birds or animals in the tree.

The tree invites you to sit with it. You sit down and feel the strength of its trunk behind your back, supporting you. Pay attention to any feelings or impressions that arise. You might feel compassion, vitality, wisdom, protection, stability, or peace. Pay attention to how you feel in this sacred place. Can you hear the song of the tree?

Spend as long as you like here. It's a safe and loving place for you to come to rest. You are supported by the strength and stability of the tree. You can be quiet here and access your inner knowing. You can bring a question or concern or ask for guidance from your tree spirit guide.

When you are ready to come back, thank the tree. Ask the tree if there is anything you can share with it. In your imagination, offer a gift to the tree of water or song or herbs. Know that you can return to this tree any time you wish. Then, return the way you came. When you have left the woods, thank the spirit of the tree and release the circle of light that surrounds you. Take a moment to wiggle your fingers and toes, and then open your eyes. Take three deep breaths. Welcome back.

It is my wish that by spending time with individual trees, time in a forest, and time with your tree spirit guide, that you will receive the gifts and blessings of these peaceful and wise beings. May you feel their strength and life within you. May they support and guide you. Spending time with trees and Nature can lead you back to the truth of your being and connect you with your inner wisdom. So often, we look for the answers outside of ourselves, when the feelings, guidance, and actions we are looking for live within us. Trees help us be aware of and enhance our communion with the flow of life force energy—*nwyfre*. They revitalize and empower us. Trees can open us to the inspiration of *awen. Awen* is a Welsh word which translates as flowing spirit or blessings of the Gods. Its creative energy offers illumination, inspiration, and wisdom. It is the source of creative power. Spending time in Nature, communing with trees, is a wonderful way to receive the inspiration of *awen* and be empowered to share your gifts with the world.

May you be blessed by the trees.

Chapter Four: Animal Wisdom

THE WISDOM OF THE Earth, of the natural world, manifests in many ways. We have looked at spending time in Nature and at building relationship with trees to access the wisdom of the Earth and your own inner wisdom. Animals also carry great wisdom that they are willing to share with us, both in the physical world and in the world of Spirit. Animals are our teachers. There are vast riches of love and power, of strength and guidance, waiting for you through animal wisdom.

ANIMALS IN NATURE

Animals live in harmony with Nature, and they can show you how to do the same. When you connect with animals, you begin to see your place in the web of life that connects us all one to another. Any thought that you are separate from or better than begins to fall away. You know that we are all connected, and our choices affect all life.

Animals can help you create a deeper relationship with Nature. Observing animals in Nature offers you the opportunity to step outside of your usual way of thinking and be still and quiet. The simple act of watching an animal can help you drop into your body and connect to your inner knowing. You must be calm and present to be around a wild animal. When you slow down, become present, and focus on being in communion with the wild animals, you find a path to the wild self within you.

Animals can bring up different feelings within us. Have you ever looked at a running horse? Seen the full flight of an eagle? Heard the chatter of sparrows? Watched a video of a cheetah on the hunt? How did it make you feel? Joyful? Empowered? Peaceful? By tuning into the energies these animals offer, you find that energy within you. It is a gift from these animals. You can also change your emotional state just by observing an animal. I remember being in hospital as a young child and watching a robin in a puddle outside my window. The presence of this bird made me feel less alone, less frightened. It brought me peace and comfort.

People often judge certain animals as being pests, dirty, carriers of disease, or just plain icky (think of how people talk about coyotes, mice, rats, seagulls, spiders, and snakes). I invite you to consider that each animal has a role, that each animal is important, and that there are no good or bad animals. Every animal deserves our respect. No matter what feeling an animal evokes in you, observing animals can teach you a great deal. They help you see how to live with an alert presence, entirely in the moment. Animals do not spend their time worrying about the future or the past. Animals are focused in the moment, aware of what they need and what is happening around them. Being present and aware, without judgment, is a great teaching of the animals.

Animal Awareness Practice

Spend time in Nature and pay attention to the animals you see. Find a place to sit and watch the animals around you. If you cannot go outside, try watching animals outside your window or on a YouTube video of wild birds or animals. Breathe in deeply three times and engage in the Grounded Flow practice. Feel the energy of the Earth and Sky flowing through you, cleansing you and filling you with light. This light flows out and creates a protective circle around you.

Listen to the birds, notice the rabbit in the field and the spider's intricate web. Watch and listen. Please ensure that you watch with soft eyes. Don't stare into the eyes of any animal or approach them with intensity. This may be interpreted at best as rude and at worst as aggressive. Be quiet in your body language and your energy. Pay attention to the life around you. Notice if any animals approach or pass by, curious about your presence. This opportunity to watch the animals can bring a deep sense of peace or freedom.

When you are ready, release the protective circle and give thanks to the animals for the experience.

Journal Questions

What animals did you see?

How did they respond to your presence?

How did they make you feel?

Did you see any insects? How did they make you feel?

When you go home, take the time to learn about the behaviour and biology of the animals you witnessed. Learning about an animal can give you insight into how they live and their place in the web of life. For example, mice provide food for many different animals. Every animal has unique skills and adaptations that help it survive and that you can learn from.

The practice of being still in Nature may invite an animal to come and visit you. I have stood silently in a winter glade listening to the quiet when a short tail weasel rocketed by me, not once but three times! It was as if he had to see for himself this unexpected person in his domain. I was sitting in a summer meadow reading a book when I sensed movement out of the corner of my eye. Looking up, I caught sight of the bushy tail of a red fox. He, too, had been intrigued and wandered up for a better look. I felt blessed by these animal encounters. When you are still and quiet, settled into your body and your being, you create an opening for others, both animal and people, to come forward.

DOMESTIC ANIMALS

An animal in your home, like a dog, cat, or rabbit, can also help you find your quiet centre. Pets often offer unconditional love. Being in their presence makes you feel better. Your pet can be your best friend or companion. Pets are like people. Some you get very close with while others are just someone to spend time with. Whatever your relationship, your pet can offer you the gift of their presence.

This is an incredible gift that should not be taken lightly. Be mindful of how you interact with your domestic animals—treat them fairly and with respect. Do not burden your pet with an expectation that they will heal you or fix you. Just be grateful to them and love them. Your gratitude, love, and respect will flow back to you. A pet can help you connect to the love within you and around you.

COMMUNING WITH YOUR PET

At a time when you will not be disturbed, sit with your pet. Do this when you can feel quiet and focus all of your attention on them. Feel the love you have for them fill up every cell in your body. Touch them with love in your hands. Feel the softness of their coat, scratch them behind their ears. Can you hear your cat purr? Does your dog want to lick your face? Connect with your pet through all of your senses. Hold your pet in the love that you feel. Always let your pet set the time and boundaries for this interaction. Do not force your pet to spend time with you or to sit on your lap. Invite them and follow their lead. Listen to what they are saying and see if you can hear what they need from you in that moment.

Journal Questions

What does it feel like to be fully present and focused on your pet?

How does your pet respond?

What if you approached all your relationships in this way (human too) fully present, connected, and listening deeply? What would change for you?

Pets help us find the joy in our being. They offer the gifts of friendship and love.

ANIMAL SPIRIT GUIDES AND MESSENGERS

There are spirit guides who help us navigate while we are here on the planet. They can be animal, plant, even mineral. The whole of the Earth speaks to us if we listen. I believe that animals can act as guides in their physical form and in the Spirit world.

Animal spirit guides are part of the cadre of helping spirits that are here to guide, protect, and heal you. Part of their purpose is to help you connect with your soul self, your inner knowing, and with the loving energy of the universe. They are beings who have your highest good and the highest good of all life in mind, and they will not coerce you, trick you, or force their own agenda on you. These helping spirits embody compassion and love and are a source of wisdom. You are protected and safe in the presence of the helping spirits.

It's important to note that when you are working with an animal spirit guide, you are not working with one animal, but with the energy or consciousness of the entire species, male and female. We don't work with a raven but with Raven. Raven represents the essence of all ravens. The spirit guide embodies all the strengths and attributes of that species. Each species or animal has its own unique gifts, its own unique perspective and way of being on the Earth, just like you. When you connect with the energy of the animal spirit guide, you can receive their strength and wisdom. When you acknowledge and listen to an animal spirit guide, you attune to their energy, to their unique spiritual vibration. Each of us has our personal energetic vibration. Everything and every being both in the physical and the non-physical or spirit world is an expression of Divine Source or the universal energy.

Animals may offer you messages to support and guide you. One way that animals offer you messages is by showing up for you in the physical world. If you notice an unusual animal, if an animal you see behaves strangely, or if you come across an animal multiple times in a brief period, you should pay attention. These kind of animal encounters have meaning. The animal may present itself in its physical form (a deer running in front of your car), or it may show up as a word, a picture, or even a feeling. However, it presents itself, Spirit is trying to talk to you.

A blue jay once found me in the middle of a treeless park, and flew around me, cawing. This was unusual, and indicative of an animal message. In time, I realized that the jay was inviting me to pay attention, to see beyond what I was seeing. Jay invited me to look up, to see not just with my physical eyes, but with all of my being—to see the layers of light and magic that exist around me. Jay invited me to consider a new perspective.

Another time I saw an owl—a rare sighting. That owl made me feel the magic that lives around me. It was an invitation to look deeper into hidden mysteries, to spend more time in prayer and meditation. One day a raven showed up, flying above me, then I found a raven feather on the ground, and later, my friend was wearing a T-shirt with a raven on it, all on the same day. For me, this was a clear sign that Raven had a message for me. I found a quiet time and connected to the energy of Raven and asked why it had come into my life. In order to connect with the energy of Raven, I was quiet. I listened and remembered how Raven felt to me. Sometimes, it can take a few days for you to understand the message. Be patient. Raven was speaking to me about possibility and what I wanted to create in my life.

I once encountered a red fox in the city. It is rare to see these shy and elusive animals where I live, so I paid attention. The red fox is particularly good at camouflage, and it can be invisible. The message for me was that I am also good at camouflage. I too can be shy and elusive, to the point of being invisible. I understood that there were times for me to stay in the background and times to show up and be seen.

An animal spirit guide may show up in the physical world or may come to you in meditations, visions, dreams, or though shamanic journeying. To connect with your guides, you need to feel calm. Using the Grounded Flow practice to enter meditation may help you settle into your body and feel calmer. In this calm state, you are more receptive to feelings, thoughts, or images that may arise. If you have trouble entering meditation, you may wish to use a practice from shamanic journeying where you begin by imagining yourself in a place in Nature that you know and love. This is a place of power and peace for you, and it may be easier to enter meditation from this place. If you wish to learn more about the shamanic journey, there are a number of excellent books on the subject.

Animal spirit guides offer guidance, inspiration, protection, and healing. They point a direction or offer perspective but will never tell you what to do. You always have free will. They can be a source of inspiration and creativity. Animal spirit guides can offer protection in the physical and non-physical or Spirit world. They can help keep you safe by triggering your intuition and causing you to stop and take notice of your situation. Animal spirit guides help heal and soothe jagged emotions and a stressed body. Animal spirit guides offer you their energy and help connect you to your power, to your connection to *nwyfre* and Spirit, helping you navigate your world and life. When you attune with an animal spirit guide, you honour and acknowledge the essence of that animal. You honour and acknowledge the energy, the strengths, and attributes that animal has. This energy or power is sometimes referred to as the animal's medicine. Your animal spirit guide will share their energy or medicine with you and help you in your daily living. These guides can help you learn about yourself and the world you live in. If they show up, in the physical world or in meditation, they are offering you an energy, a strength, or a gift. If Hawk shows up, for example, they may bring the gift of focus or vision. It is up to you to see how and where you need that gift in your life.

If an animal shows up for you, ask the animal: "What gift are you bringing?" Listen, observe, and try and feel the essence of the animal in your heart. Notice how the animal makes you feel. Reflect on what you can learn from the animal. It's always best to look to the animals themselves when trying to learn about their spiritual message or gift. Be cautious with internet as a source of information on the meaning of animal spirit guides. Many sites that claim to speak of an animal's spiritual messages only reflect cultural myths and beliefs about the animal. These can often be quite negative. If you encounter a negative interpretation of an animal, please ignore it. The spiritual attributes of an animal are always positive and always offer unconditional love. The messages they offer might not always be easy to hear or to implement, but they never present a judgment or do anything to punish you or make you feel bad. Trust your own heart and knowing, and the animal itself, for the truth of an animal's spiritual gift.

It's useful to consult biology books on animals to learn about their habits and behaviours. You can learn a lot about an animal's strengths by learning how it lives. It is for you to discover what the animal means to you spiritually. When you do this, remember not to give animals human characteristics. Animals are animals. They are not humans. Although their behaviour can serve as a metaphor for you, animals are completely themselves. What you see is the truth of who they are. As you learn about their everyday life and habits, you may learn more about their spiritual qualities and strengths. These esoteric qualities that underlie the physical animal are qualities we can connect to and draw upon. The animals are a mirror of the qualities that live within you. They can help you find and access the strengths in your own being. As you build relationship with a particular animal, over time, they will share their gifts with you and offer their teachings.

RECEIVING ANIMAL MESSAGES PRACTICE

Silently in your mind or writing in your journal, ask if there is an animal with a special message for you. Pay attention over the next week to any multiple or unusual animal sightings, whether in the physical world or in a photo or movie.

If an animal appears, get quiet and ask it what its message is for you. What is the gift it is bringing you? It could be a feeling, a word, a knowing deep within you. Be sure to ask politely. Never demand an answer. Treat the animal with love and respect. Always thank the animal for showing up, even if you don't understand the message it brings. The animal's presence is a gift in itself.

Journal Questions

Did a particular animal show up for you this past week?

Was their presence significant in any way?

What animals do you feel most drawn to? Why?

When have these animals appeared in your life?

Sometimes, I will ask for specific guidance from animals. Once I had to decide between two choices. I asked Spirit to send me an animal messenger in the form of a dove in support of one option and an owl in support of the other. The very next day, I saw two doves and seven paintings of owls—outside and inside a hospital, of all places! This information helped me gain a deeper understanding. I realized it was not an either/or choice. I needed to integrate the two options, with an emphasis on the owl aspect.

Each animal has their own unique gifts. For example, an animal who shows up for me frequently is the pine marten. The pine marten is a member of the weasel family. Many people think of the weasel's strengths as ferocity, cunning, and stealth. These are part of what weasels can offer, but what Pine Marten brought me were the gifts of curiosity and communion. Pine Marten helped me to experience a deep communion with Spirit. It was the first wild animal I called and the first one to answer.

Here's how it happened. I had been working at a hotel in one of the mountain parks. People told me there was a pine marten who lived in the woodshed, but I had been there some weeks and had never seen him (or her). The evening before I left the hotel, I asked Spirit if I could see the pine marten. On my walk the following day, there was Pine Marten, travelling along the riverbed; bright eyes looked up to me as if to say, "Well, here I am." I was overjoyed. Pine Marten had shown me that I had the ability to speak energetically with the animals, to be in communion with the wild ones. Pine Marten has crossed my path in the physical world many times since that day, each time showing me proof of our connection across species and across worlds and helping me to understand that the world is more interconnected than I ever imagined.

POWER ANIMALS

I believe that at the moment of conception, we are each given a power animal to be our ally, protector, and guide. A power animal is part of the cadre of animal spirit guides and is specific to you. They are the animal of your Spirit. Your power animal's sole purpose is to help you be fully who you are. Your power animal will help you connect to the vitality and power that flows to you from Source. They act as a guardian and protector of your connection to Source. We find aspects of our animal's strengths and attributes within ourselves. Your power animal reflects your character and personality and will reveal your strengths, attributes, and abilities. As you learn more about your power animal, you learn more about yourself.

Your power animal is an inexhaustible source of wisdom, help, protection, and power. Your power animal is a safe haven, a shoulder to lean on, and a conduit to Source or Spirit. Please note, your power animal, and any helping spirit, cannot shield you from life's challenges, but they can be a pillar of support for you as you move through these challenges. Sometimes, if you are in a difficult situation, someone yells at you, for example, you can feel your energy contract, you can lose your power. You may give away your power to someone else, through neglect, or when you feel threatened or overwhelmed. Your power animal will help you stay connected to your power. Power is not about control over another; it is about staying grounded and true to your being, connected with the vital life force energy of Spirit.

Your power animal reflects who you are. You can use their ego-neutral energy, the universal life energy of the species, in all your interactions. The power animal will share this energy with you, protect you, heal you, and guide you.

Power animals help us with the lessons we choose to learn at a soul level. So, it's helpful to build a relationship of gratitude and respect with your power animal. The personality and characteristics of your power animal are reflective of yours. As you align more closely with your power animal's behaviour and qualities, you will be more aligned with who you truly are. This alignment allows you to be your absolute best and to do things with less effort. You may feel more physical energy, increased mental alertness, and increased self-confidence the closer your relationship with your power animal becomes. The power animal strengthens your connection with your personal power and you feel more alive, more creative, and can move through the world with more confidence and ease.

It is important to remember that all power animals are equal. The mouse is as mighty as the eagle. Each has its own strengths. Power animals tend to be from the environment their person was born in, and are usually warm-blooded, as human beings are. But there are always exceptions. For example, some people born in desert climates have a reptile as a power animal. Power animals can also be mythical animals (like dragons) or extinct animals.

My power animal has helped me beyond measure and is a source of great comfort, and of laughter. Power animals tend to have a sense of humour. They do not make light of you but are incredibly good at making things lighter. They are full of joy. In time, you come to understand that your power animal is a mirror of your being—that their joy and wisdom live within you.

Meditation to Meet Your Power Animal

To begin, read through this meditation so you are familiar with it.

When you are ready, find a quiet place where you will not be disturbed. Write your intention in your journal: To connect with your power animal. Take three deep breaths. Begin the Grounded Flow practice. Feel rooted to the Earth—held and supported. Feel the warm sunlight shining on you. Imagine the energy of the Earth and Sky flowing through you. Visualize divine light filling every part of you and encompassing you in a protective circle of light. You know you are safe and protected.

Imagine you are walking in a beautiful woodland. Feel the strength and life of the trees around you. Notice if it is day or night, summer, or winter. There is a narrow path before you. You follow it. As you walk, you begin to sense the presence of many animals following you. You can't quite see them, but you sense them moving amongst the trees, flying overhead, crawling, or even swimming through the air. You remember that the standard rules of the world don't apply here, and that a whale can swim in the air. You know that any animal may be present. Perhaps every animal in the world is here, even the ones who live in the ocean or the desert, even the ones that are mythical or extinct.

You sense these animals around you, and you feel safe and supported, held in a loving embrace. The path leads you to a meadow. In the centre of the field is a slab of rock. You walk to the stone and sit; it is warm to the touch. You sense the animals have stopped on the edge of the meadow and are still hidden in the trees. Closing your eyes, take a deep breath and ask your power animal to come forward. Take another deep breath and open your eyes.

What animal stands before you?

Greet the animal. Introduce yourself and thank it for coming. Spend some time just sitting with your animal. Notice how it looks. Notice how you feel. Ask your power animal the best way to talk with or connect to them. Imagine the animal touching your heart. You can feel the animal's energy flowing to you, creating a deep and loving connection between you. Thank your power animal. When you are ready to return, ask your power animal to come with you. Then, begin to retrace your steps. Your animal may or may not walk with you, but you can feel the animal in your heart. You know that your power animal is always with you.

If you didn't see your animal, don't despair! Know that your animal is always with you and always will be. Begin to build a relationship with your power animal by asking them to send you a sign, so you know who they are. Be patient.

If several animals came forward, that's alright too. One is your power animal, and the others are animals that are helping you right now. Spend time with each and ask why they are there. Let them know why you want to work with them. Thank them for showing up. Over time, you will come to know which animal is your power animal and which are additional animal spirit guides.

When you are finished in the meadow, retrace your steps and emerge from the woods. Take a few deep breaths and then release the circle of light that surrounds you. Give thanks for this experience to the forest, to the animals, and to Spirit. You may wish to record it in your journal.

Journal Entry: Sandhill Crane

I enter the shamanic journey to find him waiting for me. He stands tall and robust, silver-grey feathers gleaming in the morning sun. I move into the glade, and he turns a great yellow eye to look at me. In the next moment, I am enfolded in his wings. He is Sandhill Crane, my power animal, and I am delighted to meet him in the Spirit world. He invites me to climb on his back, his feathers silky soft to the touch. Soaring above the trees into the blue sky, we travel far and see many things together. "I want to learn to fly," I say to him, and he replies, "You already know how." Sandhill Crane is my best friend, my protector, and my helper in all things.

Aligning With Your Power Animal

Aligning with your power animal is a way to begin creating a relationship with your animal. Aligning means that you fall into sync with the rhythms and behaviours of your animal. It is always good to learn about the biological and social patterns of the animal as a first step.

Rhythm

When is the animal active? Is it a daytime or nighttime animal? When does it rest? How does it respond to the seasons? Does it migrate? Does it hibernate?

As you approach the natural rhythm of your animal, you may find that you get more done with less effort. For example, if your animal is a daytime animal, it may be hard for you to work night shifts. (If you have to work night shifts, call on a nocturnal animal for assistance. Ask it to send you energy to help you work at night.) If your power animal hibernates in the winter, you may feel sluggish then. Winter won't be a good time for you to start major projects. If your power animal is an animal that has short bursts of intense activity and then rests, like a red fox, you may find it very hard to work in a focused way for an hour at a time. It's better to mimic the animal and work for 15 or 20 minutes, take a break or shift your focus to something else, then return to the task.

My power animal is a day-time animal. I do not work in the evening if I can avoid it. I never pulled an all-nighter at university. At one time in my life, I knew I had to spend more time in our family business and knew I would have to work both days and nights for a while. Just before I began this work, I heard an owl hooting outside the window of my suburban home. This was highly unusual, and I knew that Owl had come to offer me the gift of working at night. I drew on Owl energy to get me through the change in my routine.

Social Behaviour

Is your animal a herd animal, a pack animal, solitary, partner-bonded? Awareness of the animal's social behaviour may help you to understand aspects of yourself. For example, if your power animal is solitary, spending most of its life alone, you probably are independent and don't like to be in crowds. If your power animal lives in a herd, you will prefer working in the company of others to working alone. Sandhill Crane, my power animal, is highly social in the spring living with hundreds of thousands of cranes at the start of spring migration but lives in family units for the rest of the year. Knowing this helps me to see when I need to be with people, and when I need to be quiet in the embrace of my family. Call in the energy of other animals to support you if it's not possible to align with the social behaviour of your power animal.

Food

What does your animal eat? It is good to mimic your power animal's food choices. Keep in mind, though, that humans evolved as omnivores (we eat everything). You don't need to become a vegetarian if your animal is vegetarian, or eat meat if your animal is a carnivore. Align yourself with your animal's diet in a way that is right for you. Listen to what your body says it needs. It may, for example, need more protein. Sandhill Crane eats more protein in the spring and less in the winter. So, for me, this could be a healthy pattern to follow. Always listen to your body and trust your inner knowing about what to eat and when to eat it.

Building Relationship

Spend time with your animal in meditation or just talk to them in your head. Keep photos of the animal, or paintings, sculptures and the like, to remind you of your connection. Dance in the spirit of your power animal. How do you feel your animal would move? Pretend to be your power animal. Take the time to get to know them.

I will never forget when my Shaman was telling me about the characteristics of Sandhill Crane. He guessed that I throw my hands up in the air when I dance. He was spot on! At first, I did not think my power animal was a crane. I thought Raven was my power animal, because Raven was the animal I felt most connected to. The more I learned about the behaviour and characteristics of sandhill cranes, though, the more I realized how much I was like a crane, right down to how I dance!

One word of caution: remember that you are not your power animal. I became so deeply identified with Crane that I thought I was a crane! In time, I came to understand that Crane is one aspect of me, but not all of me. Crane came to help me with certain life lessons, but I can access the strengths of every animal. The attributes of all animals are alive within me.

Begin each day with the intention to use the energy of your power animal in your daily living. Your animal will offer you strength and vitality throughout your day. Your relationship with your power animal will become deeper and more vibrant as it develops.

OTHER ANIMAL SPIRIT GUIDES

In the teachings I have learned, you tend to have one power animal for life. That animal's role is to support you with the primary life lessons you came here to learn. This doesn't mean that other animals can't help you. In fact, your power animal will call other animals to your aid when you need their specific attributes or strengths, as happened to me with Owl. You can also call upon other animals yourself if you feel you need their power. For example, you may be facing a demanding situation, and need the ferocity of Wolverine to get you through it. If you don't know what you need, ask your power animal. They can show you, or help you figure it out.

It is possible that your power animal could change if your focus in your soul's life learning changes. We have free will and can make different choices.

Don't be afraid to ask your power animal for any kind of help or protection. They are there for you in every way. If I'm feeling difficult emotions or experiencing a challenging situation, I offer it to my power animal, and Sandhill Crane helps to resolve and heal the situation.

Animals are a part of Nature. Animals in the wild, pets in your home, and animal spirit guides that live in the spiritual realm can all help and support you to connect with your inner knowing and with the wisdom of Nature. Animals can help you to be fully present, to be still, to listen deeply, and to move with awareness through your daily life. They offer you unconditional love, support, inspiration, and compassion. Treat the animals, in your inner and outer worlds, with love, compassion, and respect. Your love and gratitude will be offered back to you.

Chapter Five: Earth Rhythm Wisdom

Tʜᴇ ɢʟᴏᴀᴍɪɴɢ ᴛʜᴀᴛ ʜᴇʀᴀʟᴅꜱ the setting of the sun...
Bathing in the light of a full moon...
The smell of wet Earth...
Wind rustling the leaves of a tree...
Crunching leaves underfoot on a crisp autumn day...
The sound of rain on your roof...
The quiet of snow falling...
Crackling flames sending sparks into the night sky...
Your garden on a warm summer's day...

All these experiences reflect the ever-changing rhythm of Nature. Each day and every season offer gifts of beauty, peace, and teachings that can enhance your life.

In Nature, there is life and death, seasons and turnings, beginnings and endings that reflect your own complex life. Your well-being is heightened when you are in touch with the natural rhythms of the Earth.

I feel that our society has lost touch with the Earth. Most of us live in an urban environment. We usually depend on a clock to wake us and to tell us when to sleep and eat. We may no longer listen to our bodies or pay attention to the movement of the sun. We often rush through our days, focused on the tasks we need to complete and the responsibilities we need to live up to, and we miss the subtle nuances that Nature offers us. We experience the world through our thinking or logical mind, and we miss the wonder and magic of life. We have forgotten the ancient wisdom of our ancestors that connects us to our truth and to all life on the planet. This is a terrible loss. But it can be repaired!

Inner Knowing

When you are in relationship with Earth rhythms, you become aware of your sacred connection with Spirit, the Divine Source that connects us all in the web of life. When you live attuned to your personal rhythms and to the rhythm of your surroundings, you know you are a part of everything, and you no longer feel a sense of separation from yourself, from the Earth, or from Spirit. You can receive the many gifts and blessings of Nature. Aligning with this life force energy enables you to live with honour and respect for all life, including your own. Spending time in the natural world helps you to allow the stream of well-being that is available to you from Spirit. Engaging with Earth rhythms helps foster this connection and enables you to move from your thinking mind and into the heart of who you are. This connection creates a flow of meaning and purpose for your life. Nature provides nourishment for the soul and the body. Creativity, inspiration, and new ideas are birthed from the deep well of the soul. Nature helps you access these qualities within you and is a path to seeing with your inner sight.

Nature helps you discover wholeness, peace, and beauty, within and without.

As you move to wholeness, you can more readily offer your unique gifts to the world. Through this relationship you empower yourself and all life. Nature is a gateway for Spirit to work through you.

Celtic Wisdom

The ancient Celts lived in a sacred landscape. They considered the land and everything in it—rocks, trees, water, the air—to be enlivened with Spirit, with the Divine. The land was the Goddess, the Great Mother. Gods and Goddesses inhabited the springs, rivers, wells, caves, and crossroads. The Celts held a deep reverence for the land, sea, and sky. They lived attuned with their surroundings.

They moved in rhythm with the rising and setting of the sun and moon, with the changing seasons.

The Celts marked the turning of the year with celebrations that honoured their physical and spiritual life. The year turns and marks the increasing and decreasing sunlight, the seasons, the movement of animals, the movement of the moon, and the growth and death of plants and crops. Celtic people knew that their lives depended on these seasonal rhythms and saw themselves as part of the turning wheel of the year.

Today we can mark the turning of the year with the seasonal solar wheel (See image at end of chapter). The wheel reflects the Earth's rhythms and divides the year based on the turning of the sun, reflecting the solstices and equinoxes. The solstices are the longest and the shortest days and the equinoxes are times when day and night are in balance. The seasonal wheel is divided into the four seasons.

The Earth's rhythms teach us about the rhythms in our own lives. All life on Earth turns around the sun. Your life and the life of the land, the plants and the animals are intertwined. We can find teachings, wisdom, and strength within the patterns of the seasons.

The turning of the day is also reflected in the wheel. The day turns from sunrise to noon and from sunset to nightfall. Each part of the day offers wisdom and teachings. Day follows day in an eternal cycle. The days flow into the turning of the seasons. The rhythm of the Earth reflects and informs the rhythm of the day, the year, and your life from birth to death. Each season, each sunrise offers insight into your living.

The year turns from spring to summer, summer to autumn, autumn to winter, and begins again. All things are born; all things die; all life is renewed. You can see the turning over the course of a year—growth, harvest, death, decay, and rebirth. Creation and destruction move together to form our world. Life does not flow in an unchanging endless circle but moves in a spiral where each turning takes us deeper into the mystery and offers us new insight and new growth. The Earth can guide us through life transitions—the birth, death, and rebirth that occur on so many levels in our lives.

We are all aware that this is the reality for our physical body. We are born, we live, we die, and our bodies return to the Earth. Only the soul is eternal. The seasonal cycle is also reflected in various aspects of our lives. Destruction may show up as a challenge that we experience—illness, job loss, divorce, or the death of a loved one. We will all experience challenges many times in our life. Nature and the Earth's rhythms show us that after an ending, there is a beginning. Renewal often arises from the setbacks in our lives; a new opportunity may present itself, we may re-evaluate priorities, or we may have a spiritual awakening. This is the cycle of creation, destruction, and renewal in action in our daily living.

Earth rhythm wisdom can help you understand this cycle and realize that nothing is permanent. There will be good times and bad. There will be hope and despair. The world around us changes, the circumstances of our lives change, even our bodies change, yet beneath it all is an eternal truth. Your soul self is eternal. There is a divine intelligence or Spirit that underlies all these rhythms and challenges that is eternal, too. The turning wheel connects us all one to another, people, Nature, and Spirit, and we grow and change with each turning. Grief, joy, love, and fear are all held within the wheel. Living in relationship with Earth rhythms help us understand what it is to be alive and how to engage with the creative life force of this world.

There is a rhythm of giving and receiving, of creating and destroying, of gathering knowledge in and sharing it, of beginning and ending, that is reflected in the turning seasons. In every moment, Nature is offering you gifts of communion and wisdom.

Circles and Directions

The Seasonal Solar Wheel is a turning circle. This circle is a symbol of unity and wholeness, reflecting the cycles of Nature and our lives. The Seasonal Solar Wheel holds infinite possibilities and the interconnection of many different energies you can draw on and work with. The energies of the four seasons are associated with the energies of the elements of Earth, Air, Fire, and Water and with the four cardinal directions of North, East, South, and West. The four directions and the four elements each feel different and offer unique teachings that help you connect with the land and your inner Self.

In this chapter, we will explore the qualities associated with each season and discover how these qualities can help you in your daily living. These concepts reflect the experience and teachings of my Northern European ancestors and druidry. If you live in the tropics, the seasons may be much more subtle or reflect differences such as a wet or dry season. Other cultures may have different associations or correspondences. For example, the elements may sit in different places, or they may have different animals associated with the directions.

I will share the teachings that I live and work with. I believe these teachings will help you build a relationship with the Earth in your own way, a way that reflects the land you live on. The teachings are a gateway to your unique understanding and will offer you practices that you can use no matter where you live.

What I share is just an entry point for you to begin your spiritual journey with Earth rhythm wisdom. It is up to you to discover your personal relationship and correspondences with the land you live on.

Earth Rhythm Correspondences

Life moves in a circle. You stand in the centre and can learn how to be in relationship with its different energies and aspects. The sun is at the centre of the solar wheel. Your soul is at the centre of your life. With you at the centre is Spirit Source. From Source emanates the creative life force energy of *nwyfre* that underlies and supports all life. You are part of that connected web of energy. Everything has Spirit and energy, and because you have Spirit and energy too, you can connect with and be in relationship with them. You can learn to live in balance and harmony with all aspects of the solar wheel and all aspects of yourself. You can learn how to work with, move across, and integrate the energies of the seasonal solar wheel.

The wheel shows you how to be in relationship with yourself, with other people, and with the Earth. It helps you to see beyond how you usually look at your life, to see the greater life—the complexity and layers of life that exist in the seen and unseen worlds. The wheel and its associated energies or correspondences reflect rhythms of the Earth and of your life, energies that you can draw on, learn from, and integrate into your daily living. You can connect to the distinct aspects of your being (body, mind, heart, and spirit) through the spirit of the elements, the spirit of the directions, and the spirit of the seasons.

Changing Seasons

The seasons do not change abruptly from one day to the next. Instead, they flow gradually one into the other. This means you may experience the energies of two seasons at once. The time when seasons flow one into another is a liminal time.

It is an in-between place, both physically and spiritually, when the land and your life are shifting, moving from one energy to the next. They are no longer what they were, and they are not yet what they will become.

In Celtic spirituality, liminal time and place is where the boundary between the seen and unseen worlds, between the physical and spiritual world, is thin. A thin place or time is a threshold between the physical and spiritual world. It is a magical time or place where you can sense that you are part of something greater than yourself and access your connection with the sacred.

You can access the qualities and the energies of any season at any time of the year. In truth, you move through the energies of the seasons every single day, from sunrise to noon to sunset to darkness. These energies or correspondences are always present and available to you. When you seek to balance the energies of the seasons within you, when you build that relationship with the seasons, you can access what you need to support and empower you in your daily living.

Spring

In spring, the Earth awakens from a winter slumber. Life stirs across the land, the days grow longer, babies are born, and new shoots poke through the soil. You can feel spring in your physical body as your body adapts metabolically to the increasing sunlight. You can feel it in your emotions as a sense of hope. You can feel it mentally, as you plan out a garden or summer holiday, and you can feel like you are coming alive in your Spirit, just as the Earth is coming alive.

Spring is a time of new growth and new beginnings. It is a time of planting and planning. You welcome the burgeoning sunlight and the awakening of the Earth as a new growing season begins. Spring flowers, planting seeds, the birth of animals, and planning a garden are all things you may associate with spring.

Meditation: Meeting the Spirit of Spring

I invite you to use your imagination. As you move through this guided visualization to connect with the energies of spring, pay attention to how you feel.

Imagine you stand in the dimness at the end of a spring night. It is cool, and you shiver in the predawn darkness. The light begins to bleed over the edge of the horizon—a deep band of pink that expands upward ever so slowly. You watch the colour change, softening to lighter shades of pink and orange. The air smells sweet and clean. As the night fades, the light brings the promise of a new day, of new possibilities. You are in that place between day and night, that place where this world and the world of Spirit are close together. This is a liminal space.

It feels like it is taking forever for the sun to rise. And then the dawn breaks over the horizon, flooding the world with light.

You hear birds greeting the new day with their song.

A bird in flight seems to beckon to you from the sky.

The pale glow of early morning lights up the flowers in the grass at your feet. The flowers give off a faint scent—the scent of hope.

The dawn brings with it a gentle breeze, carrying stories of people and places far away. Your worries and cares are taken by the wind, and you stand refreshed and renewed. It is a new day, full of possibility. The new day carries the spirit of spring.

What feeling does the season offer you?

When you are ready, take a deep breath and return to the here and now. Write down any thoughts, feelings, or impressions that came up for you during this meditation. Journaling after a meditation can help you discover patterns and insights.

Correspondences of Spring

In this section, we will explore the different correspondences associated with spring—its archetypal associations. An *archetype* is a universal recurring pattern, idea, or energy that is associated with a particular concept. The archetypal associations for spring and the other seasons are an entry point for you to develop your unique relationship with the Earth. I invite you to go beyond these correspondences to discover your own personal associations with each season.

Spring is associated with childhood and youth. It is a time of fertility, when masculine and feminine energy come together in a sacred union to create new life. Sunlight increases and awakens the greening of the Earth, the awakening of life. You can feel new life awaken in you as you are called to be a part of the dance of life.

Direction: East

The **East** is the place of the rising sun. It is the place of new beginnings. Most obviously, it is the beginning of a new day, but it can also mean childhood—the beginning period of your life—or the start of a new project, job, a new career, a new endeavour. Spring invites you to begin anew and to bring a sense of child-like wonder to your life. It is a breath of fresh air.

Practice of Connection:

If possible, stand facing East and greet the sun each morning (even if you are not awake for sunrise). Engage in the Grounded Flow practice. Give thanks for your day. Feel or imagine the sun's rays warming and energising you. Feel into your centre and ask what you need this day and what the world needs from you today. Take your time. When you have finished, thank the direction and release your protective circle in the usual way.

Element: Air

A word about the four elements. Fire, Water, Air, and Earth are inspirited. Each has its own energy and spirit. Your body is made up of the elements, as is everything in the physical world. All the elemental energies are part of the physical realm and work to support you here in this physical world. When you consciously engage with the energy of any element, its power is activated.

Approach the four elements with gratitude and treat them with respect. The elements carry both creative energy and destructive energy. They bring healing, renewal, and cleansing. But, as anyone who has experienced a fire, a tornado, an earthquake, or a flood knows, they can also bring death and destruction. By connecting with the elements, you can learn how to integrate all their energies within yourself for balance, vitality, and well-being.

We tend to feel most connected to one or two of the elements. Ultimately, over the course of the year, I hope you can begin to find balance and deepen your connection with all four of them.

The Element of **Air** is associated with spring.

Air is your breath and the sacred breath of Spirit. Air is essential for life. It is the wind that brings new life and new inspiration. That wind can be fierce enough that you must lean into it, or it can be a gentle breeze at your back. The wind carries birds on the wing, seeds, water, snow, warmth, and freshness.

The wind teaches you to be a conduit of Spirit and to be fierce and gentle as needed. The wind brings the gift of clarity of thought. It carries away what you need to let go of, bringing in creativity. Air is associated with illumination and communication.

Practice of Connection:

If possible, go outside on a windy day. If that's not possible, imagine you are on a high mountain top where you can feel the wind on your face. Engage in the Grounded Flow practice. Pay attention to the wind.

Is it warm or cold?

Imagine you can taste the wind. What does it taste like?

Speak your name to the wind. Introduce yourself. The wind carries messages and stories. Wind is a bearer of change. Does the wind have a message for you?

What would you like to release to the wind?

What would you like to receive from the wind?

What does the wind need from you?

Does the wind offer you clarity of thought or mind?

Imagine that you have wings and can soar on the wind. When you are ready, float gently down to the Earth. Thank the element of Air and release your protective circle. Write down any thoughts or feelings that arose in your journal.

Animal: Hawk of the Dawn

In the teachings I have received, Hawk is the animal that lives in the East. Hawk has sharp vision and can see far. Hawk helps you see the bigger picture of your life. Hawk can also see the tiniest movement on the ground. Hawk can help you find a unique perspective, create a clear vision for the future, and notice any details in your life that you need to be aware of. Spring and Hawk offer clarity, focus, and understanding.

Hawk invites you to take a step back and create a vision for your life. Spring is the time to celebrate the rebirth of the Earth. There is a quickening of the Earth. You feel it in the land, and you feel it in your being. It is a time of planting and new beginnings. It is time to plant the seeds of your inner vision.

Journal Questions

What creative expression is awakening in you, that seeks to grow and flourish along with the plants and animals? A new project? Artistic expression, like playing music or writing? Fostering your relationships?

What vision for your life can you see through Hawk's eyes?

Does Hawk help you see your life from a different perspective?

Tree of Spring

The tree that I personally associate with spring is the Schubert's chokecherry. This tree is a bright spirit, vibrant and alive. In the spring its leaves open green, then turn red over the summer. This tree is covered in sweet smelling blossoms every spring, and one of my spring rituals is to lie beneath its branches and enjoy the beauty of this tree. The blossoms smell like spring to me.

Journal Questions

Which aspect of spring do you most enjoy? Go through your senses and see if you can identify the joys spring brings you through each of the senses: sight, sound, smell, taste and touch.

Where else do you find beauty in your life?

What refreshes and renews your spirit?

Spring Equinox

Northern Hemisphere: March 21/22

Southern Hemisphere: September 21/22

The spring equinox is the time when the day and night are in perfect balance. Every day after the spring equinox, the light increases until it reaches its maximum power at the summer solstice. The balance of light and dark invite you to consider the balance of opposites in your life. The balance of joy and sorrow, giving and receiving, striving and surrender. It is a good opportunity to see where you may be out of balance and what steps you need to take to restore balance in your physical, emotional, and intellectual life. Balance is not a steady state. It is always in motion and depends on the needs of the day. Balance is also about accepting that supposed opposites co-exist at the same time. You can experience joy and sorrow in the same day and even in the same moment. The equinox shows you that opposites are in truth simply different aspects or expressions of the whole. You can unite all aspects of your being. The equinox invites you to integrate perceived opposing energies. This teaching allows you to feel compassion and acceptance of people who may hold viewpoints or ideas that are different from your own. Each person is a different expression of Source or the Divine. We are all part of something bigger than ourselves, and each person has a gift and an energy to offer that makes the world whole.

The equinox is a good time to stop and consider what you need more or less of in your life.

Your Personal Correspondences

I invite you to discover your personal connections or correspondences with the seasons, starting with spring.

When does the first bird of spring appear?

Can you sense when the Earth is awakening?

What tree opens its leaves first? Or last?

When do the first flowers appear?

When do the animals come out of hibernation or when do birds return from migration?

What changes occur in your life with the coming of spring?

What feelings come up in this season?

What stars or constellations are prevalent in the night sky?

What tree or animal is symbolic of spring for you?

You may want to jot these observations into a notebook or write them in your calendar. If you can, start noticing a tree or plant on a daily walk or out of your window. Over time, you will notice subtle changes: what the tree is up to and how it moves through the seasons.

You may wish to ask for an offering from Nature that is symbolic of the energy of spring for your sacred gift box.

Honouring the Season of Spring

Plant a seed, inside or outside, and help it grow. Fostering another living being creates a connection. Sing to, pray over, and talk to your plant every day. In time, you will begin to feel a connection with this plant. Here are some other suggestions:

- Watch the sunrise.

- Practice a breathing meditation.

- Sing or chant to engage with your sacred breath and with Air.

- Hang a spring wreath or place a spring candle on your table.

- Observe the spring equinox.

These practices are not meant to be tasks that you check off a list but a way to help you create a deep and loving connection with the Earth and with the qualities of the season.

Remember, we do not take from our Earth, but share with the Earth. As the Earth gives and support us, we too can give love and support the Earth. We can offer our time, our love, our attention, our songs and prayers. We can offer financial support for reforestation or animal welfare. We can make choices in our daily living that support the Earth.

May you receive the blessings of spring, of Air, of new beginnings.

Summer

Summer is the time to celebrate the strength of the sun. The sun is at its greatest power, fueling life on the Earth and offering that life-giving energy to you in your life and work. All the world is green, lush, and alive. All the food you eat carries the energy of the Sun. The fire of the sun mirrors the fire of your Spirit. Summer offers you the energy to take action to fulfill the vision you created in the spring. Summer offers an opportunity to embrace the creativity and abundance of life and to enhance your vitality. Summer is associated with adulthood, a time when you have strength and power. It is a time of commitment and accomplishment.

Summer is a time of expansion. It is a time to celebrate love and communion with your soul, with your loved ones, and with Nature. You revel in the light and in the power of creation. You manifest your hopes and dreams. It is a time to celebrate and be joyful as you receive the blessings of the light.

Meditation: Meeting the Spirit of Summer

Find a comfortable seat. Take three deep cleansing breaths. Imagine yourself in a mountain meadow. The noon sun shines down on you. The mountains rise like rocky sentinels around you. The tall peaks are mirrored in a small, crystal-clear lake before you. The meadow is alive with life. You hear bees buzzing, see the explosion of colour from the flowers, and smell the warm grass. A soft breeze caresses your face. At your feet, wild strawberries grow—tiny red treasures. You pick a handful to eat. Their sweetness explodes in your mouth. They taste like summer.

Out of the corner of your eye, you see a deer and her fawn grazing on the far side of the meadow. A squirrel chitters at you from the nearby trees, and a golden eagle soars above you. You feel the life and abundance of the meadow in your heart and soul, filling you with joy and energy as you hike up to the top of the mountain. The world is spread before you. You feel a deep sense of accomplishment. Today is the summer solstice, the longest day of the year, and you have hours of daylight left to enjoy this perfect summer day. What feeling does the season offer you?

When you are ready, take a deep breath and return to the here and now.

Write down any thoughts, feelings, or impressions that came up for you during this meditation.

Correspondences of Summer

Direction: South

South is the place of the midday sun, of summer, of growth and creativity, of fire and transformation. South is associated with purification, overcoming obstacles, self-sufficiency, and adulthood. It is a place of inner strength, confidence, and accomplishment.

Practice of Connection:

If possible, stand facing South at midday. Engage in the Grounded Flow practice. Feel the strength and vitality of the sun. Lift your arms to the sun. This is a great pick me up if you feel tired.

Take your time. When you have finished, thank the direction, and release your protective circle in the usual way.

Element: Fire

The element of Fire is associated with summer.

Fire gives you the vitality, energy, passion, and the strength of the sun. We gather around a fire to share its warmth and protection. The hearth is the heart of every home. Fire offers light and invokes enthusiasm and energy in your life. It is instrumental in healing and renewal. We sterilize surgical instruments and cauterize wounds with heat. Fire offers purification as it burns away the deadwood of thoughts and beliefs that no longer serve you. From the ashes, new creative energy and new perspective are born. Fire transforms.

Fire's transformative power is needed in Nature. Fire revitalizes and renews the land. A lodgepole pine will only release its seeds when it is brushed by fire. But fire that is too hot, fire out of balance, will destroy, as when a forest fire burns so hot that it kills all the forest's trees. The same is true in our lives—too much fiery passion can lead to heated responses and scorched earth in our relationships. We can burn the candle at both ends, be consumed by our passions, and suffer from burnout.

Fire heals and Fire destroys. The heat of a fever cures us, but it can also kill us. Fire teaches us responsibility. It teaches us to think, and to temper our actions with insight.

Fire always offers hope of rebirth. Even when the forest or our relationships have been destroyed, there is new growth that arises from the ashes.

Practice of Connection:

Before beginning this practice, remember that Fire is powerful, and you need to feel comfortable working with it. Always consider safety when working with candles or campfires. Make sure your candle is in a fireproof holder and will not tip over. Ensure that there are no curtains or hanging objects near your candle. Never leave a candle unattended. Have water nearby as an extra measure of safety.

If you do not feel comfortable working with Fire, then don't. You can imagine looking into a candle flame or choose not to do this practice.

To begin, engage in the Grounded Flow practice. Light a candle. Set an intention to receive healing light and energy from the element of Fire. When you are ready, gaze into the flames. Visualize healing energy flowing into you from the flame. Feel the flame's strength and vitality. What gift does Fire offer you? Does it bring a feeling or an inspiration? Does it offer power? Peace? Maybe it gives you creativity or transformation. Do you need this intensity to fuel your goals, or do you need less heat in your life?

If at any time you feel fearful or uncomfortable, stop what you're doing. Blow out the candle and feel the Earth beneath you offering strength and stability. Take a few deep cleansing breaths and let your breath anchor you in the here and now.

When you feel complete, thank the element of Fire, and extinguish the candle. Release your circle of light. Write down in your journal any thoughts or feelings that arose.

The Great Stag

The animal associated with Summer is the Stag. Stag lives in the south. They are majestic beings to behold, with impressive antlers and a ruff of hair around their neck. The Stag roars during mating season, a sound that echoes in your bones and enlivens your spirit. Stag is prepared to challenge and defend, moving with grace and poise. Stag is considered one of the oldest animals in Celtic traditions and is seen as a messenger from the unseen world. Stag is a virile and powerful animal who offers the gifts of independence, strength, and dignity. You can draw on these attributes to help you accomplish your goals and empower you in life. Stag inspires integrity and confidence.

Journal Questions

What has fired your passions?

What needs to be nurtured in your life?

What steps do you need to take to realize your vision?

What aspects of your life would benefit from increased confidence, power, or integrity?

Tree of Summer

The tree that I associate with summer is the burr oak. This tree grows in my backyard and often struggles to survive in my climate zone. For me, this tree speaks of tenacity and strength. It is slow and steady in its growth. It is a tree to plant for future generations. It carries ageless wisdom and invites me to see beyond what I think is possible. It is a living testament of Spirit at work in my life.

Journal Questions

What wisdom does the burr oak offer you?

Where could you benefit from the inner strength of the burr oak?

Where do you see Spirit at work in your life?

Summer Solstice

Northern Hemisphere: June 21/22

Southern Hemisphere: December 21/22

The summer solstice is the longest day of the year. The sun has reached its maximum power. The solstice marks another turn in the seasonal wheel and is an opportunity to acknowledge the deep and mysterious connection between your life and the rhythm of the seasons. It is a day to celebrate the light and the vibrant energy that is available to you in your life. You enjoy the light and power of creation as you take action to manifest your hopes and dreams. As the energy of the sun opens the heart of the Earth, may you open your heart to the joy, passion, love, and abundance that surrounds you.

How can you celebrate the height of summer?

Your Personal Correspondences

Write down everything that summer means to you. What do you think about when you think of summer? Include childhood experiences as well as what it means to you right now.

Pay attention to the changes that have occurred for the special tree or plant you befriended in the spring. Does the tree feel different now?

Continue to record your observations of how Nature changes through this season.

What animal or tree do you associate with summer?

Ask Nature for a gift for your sacred gift box that is symbolic of summer.

Honouring the Season of Summer

- Visit a park or your garden and notice the beauty and abundance of the vegetables and flowers growing there.

- Place a bouquet of flowers on your table.

- Cook a meal filled with fresh vegetables and herbs.

- Go on a picnic with friends.

- Sit around an outdoor fire.

- Engage in a summer pursuit like hiking, boating, swimming, or playing an outdoor game or sport.

- Hang a summer wreath or place a summer candle on your table.

- Walk barefoot.

- Observe the summer solstice.

May you receive the blessings of summer, of Fire and vitality.

Autumn

Autumn brings warm days and cool nights, crisp apples, and fields of wheat. It is the time of the harvest, a time of thanksgiving for gifts and blessings received from the Earth and in your life. It is the end of the growing season. You harvest the fruit of your labour and can see the results of your actions over the year. It is a time of fulfillment and reflection. You stand at the threshold of the dark time of the year. For many, it's a time of sadness as we mourn our lost dreams or the dying back of the land. At this time of the year, the light is waning, and the land is preparing for the deep sleep of winter.

Autumn corresponds with the moon, maturity, and sunset. It is a time when the veil between this world and the Spirit world thins, and you can connect with your ancestors.

Autumn is a time to honour your ancestors. You can feel ancestral wisdom in your blood and bones. You carry a genetic memory—a spiritual connection that allows a remembering of ancient knowledge, truth, and kinship.

Autumn is a time of maturity and claiming the wisdom of the elders.

Meditation: Meeting the Spirit of Autumn

Settle into your body. Take three deep cleansing breaths. Imagine that you are walking in a beautiful meadow. The sun is low on the horizon. It is twilight, that special time between day and night. Pale sunshine slants across the field from a bright blue sky. The tall grass dances in the breeze, heavy with seeds. A few trees dot the meadow, their branches laden with red apples. You pluck an apple from a tree, offering your thanks for the tree's gift. The apple crunches as you bite into it and taste its sweetness.

The brambles are an explosion of blackberries. Everywhere you look you see the abundance of summer's growth. You hear the soft rush of water and move towards it. You discover a stream running through a stand of trees. You decide to follow the stream for a while. You can smell the water and the damp earth. Fallen leaves rustle underfoot as you walk. The changing leaves on the trees glow red and gold, like fairy lights. The warmth of the day is fading with the setting sun, and you are glad for your warm jacket. Your steps turn you back towards your home, where there is a warm fire and hot tea waiting for you.

What feeling does the season offer you?

When you are ready, take a deep breath and return to the here and now. Write down any thoughts, feelings, or impressions that came up for you during this meditation.

Correspondences of Autumn

Direction: West

West is the place of the setting sun and completion. It is the time of maturity and reflection. West is associated with Water of every kind—rain, seas, and fog—and with our watery emotions, our dream life, and the subconscious. The West represents intuition, emotion, fluidity, and letting go. Autumn is a time when we can see our death on the horizon.

Practice of Connection:

If possible, stand facing West at sunset. Engage in the Grounded Flow practice. Engage with the ever-changing palette of the sky as the day fades to darkness. As the sun drops below the horizon, can you see the moon rising?

When you have finished, thank the direction, and release your protective circle in the usual way.

Journal Questions

Reflect on your day. What are you grateful for?

What gifts did the sunset bring?

Record any feelings, insights, or understanding.

Element: Water

Water is essential for all life, and is associated with dreams, intuition, and emotion. Water invites you to feel your emotions and let them be a guide to your truth. Flowing water has tremendous power. It can erode rock and carve stone. It can dissolve and wash away obstacles and barriers. Water flows where it is needed. Water helps you to find the flow, the rhythm of your living. Water soothes, heals, and cleanses you.

Practice of Connection:

Next time you have a bath or a shower, thank the Water for its cleansing and blessing. Imagine the Water is alive with healing and soothing energy. Feel the Water that flows within your body. Try this for a week and notice how you feel.

You are a force of Nature, like the elements. Is there an aspect of your life that is stagnant and would benefit from the flowing energy of Water?

Chart the flow of your subconscious mind with a dream journal. Recording your dreams can help you gain self-awareness and offer insight from your subconscious about your thoughts, feelings, and beliefs.

Salmon Wisdom

The animal associated with the West is Salmon. In the Druidic tradition, the salmon is the oldest animal. It is very sacred. The main attribute of Salmon is wisdom. Salmon moves in the watery world of the subconscious. Salmon can find its way home across the widest sea. Salmon creates new life, and in death feeds and nurtures the Earth and animals, like bears and eagles, who feed on their carcasses. Salmon DNA is found in the trees near their spawning grounds. The river and the salmon bring life and nourishment for all beings. The river of life can take you far from your starting place and Salmon can help you remember your beginnings and find wisdom in your journey. Salmon shows you how to navigate the watery emotions you experience and to trust your deepest instinct and intuition.

Journal Questions

Is there some part of your Soul that longs to go home?

How can you find inspiration and wisdom in your journey?

What does Salmon have to teach you?

The Tree of Autumn

The tree I associate with autumn is the laurel leaf willow. The willow is a water loving tree and likes to grow in damp ground. It is flexible yet strong. It bends to the force of the gale and gives up its branches freely to the wind. It is self-pruning. Willow carries prayers and messages to my ancestors. It shows me how to stand with grace in life's storms. Willow teaches how to let go and not be too attached to any particular "branch," and how to feel and move with your emotions as they flow.

Journal Questions

Where in your life would it serve you to be more flexible and to let go?

Are you moving in the flow of life?

Are you in touch with your emotions?

Autumn Equinox

Northern Hemisphere: September 21/22

Southern Hemisphere: March 21/22

The autumn equinox is the time when the day and the night are balanced. You stand at a perfect balance at the threshold of the dark time of the year. Every day after the equinox, the light will decrease until it reaches its minimum power at the winter solstice. The balance of light and dark invites you to consider the balance of opposites in your life. The equinox teaches that there will always be light and dark in your life. There will always be challenges. The equinox invites you to respond to these challenges in a balanced way, to know in your heart that darkness has a role to play and that the light always returns.

Do you respond to challenges in a balanced way? How do you balance the abundance of the harvest with the dying of the land?

Your Personal Correspondences

Continue to pay attention to the plants and animals around you and how they change during autumn. Record these changes in your journal.

What tree or animal is symbolic of autumn for you?

What do you love most about autumn?

Take stock of your life and achievements during autumn:

What are you proud of this year?

What needs to be uprooted, discarded, changed?

You may want to consider collecting a gift from Nature for your sacred gift box that is a symbol of autumn.

Honouring the Season of Autumn

- Pick apples in an orchard.

- Bake a pie or make jam.

- Harvest your garden.

- Watch the sunset.

- Write down everything you are grateful for.

- Drink water to nurture your body and your emotional health.

- Research your ancestors.

- Share memories and stories of loved ones who have passed.

- Observe the autumn equinox.

May you receive the blessings of autumn, of Water and wisdom.

Winter

I love the deep quiet of winter. Icy winds from the north scour the land and your soul, cleansing and clearing you. There is a clarity and a sharpness that lives in the winter wind that awakens and heals. Winter is associated with old age, death and darkness. Winter allows you to go deep within, to rest and be quiet. It is a time of stillness. In the peaceful dark of winter, you rest, grounded in the Earth, and receive inspiration from the well of your soul. Creation is birthed in the darkness. The Earth slumbers beneath blankets of snow, and who knows what possibility will be born in the spring? The seed lies under the snow, waiting for the light of the new year. Winter is a time of incubation. In the long dark, new ideas are conceived. Winter is a time of quiet, contemplation, and inspiration.

Meditation: Meeting the Spirit of Winter

Take a moment to find a comfortable seat. Take a few deep cleansing breaths and settle into your body. Let your mind be quiet. Imagine that you are walking in a forest of evergreens in the mountains. Night has fallen. The wind sighs in the trees like whispers from Spirit. Your breath turns to fog in the frosty air. Tiny points of light from the distant stars spangle the black velvet sky. The liquid light of a full moon illuminates your path, and the snow sparkles like diamonds. Everything seems sharper and clearer in the cold night air.

You burrow into your warm cloak. Soon you reach a clearing in the forest. From here, you can see the mountains rise around you, their dark shapes dressed in winter white. The world is black and white and shades of grey. The beauty astounds you. Nothing seems to move or breathe in the deep quiet of the night. Nothing but you. All you can hear are your own footsteps, muffled by the deep snow. The Earth sleeps under a white mantle. The deep quiet of winter fills your soul with peace. You pause to drink in the beauty of the night. You rest in the womb of the earth, quiet and waiting for the light.

What feeling does the season offer you?

When you feel ready, take a few deep breaths and open your eyes, returning to the here and now.

Write down any thoughts, feelings, or impressions that came up for you during this meditation.

Correspondences of Winter

Direction: North

North is the place of darkness and death. It is the place of Earth and winter. North is a time of silence, stillness and peace. It is the time of midnight. Midnight is a liminal time, an in-between time, when the veil between the physical world and the world of Spirit is thin. The North offers wisdom, inspiration and resilience.

Journal Questions

What physical support and abundance have you received in your life?

How would you benefit from a period of silence and rest?

What seed of an idea arises from the depths of your soul, waiting in the dark rich loam of your being to be born in the spring?

Practice of Connection:

If it is safe to do so, go outside and stand facing north at midnight. If this is not possible, do this practice inside or imagine it is midnight.

Engage in the Grounded Flow practice. How does this time of day feel? Sense the strength of the Earth and the vast expanse of the night sky. Can you find the moon? How is the night sky different from the daytime? What feeling does it evoke? Vincent van Gogh wrote in a letter to his brother that "the starry night is more alive and richly coloured than the day." Is that your experience?

If you can, do this practice a few times, at different stages of the moon. Notice how it feels to bathe in the moonlight. How does the full moon feel? Does the new moon feel different to you? Pay attention to how you feel, not to what your culture says about the full and new moon. Can you notice any changes from the waxing and the waning moon?

Take your time. When you have finished, thank the direction, and release your protective circle in the usual way.

Element: Earth

Earth offers stability, strength, and foundation. It is associated with the physical world and invites you to care for your physical needs. Nurturing and abundance are aspects of Earth. Earth offers cycles of change and transformation, growth and decay, of birth and death.

Practice of Connection:

If possible, find a rocky outcropping or large boulder that you can sit on. If this is not possible, find a stone or pebble that you can hold in your hand. Engage in the Grounded Flow practice. Ask the rock if you may sit with or carry it. If you feel the answer is yes, thank it for its help. Feel the rock beneath you or in your hand. What feeling does it evoke in you? Can you hear the language of the stone? Is it words? A feeling? Do you feel a connection with the Earth? When you are ready, thank the element and the stone and release your protective circle. Ask if the stone is meant to stay with you or be returned to Nature.

The Great Bear

The animal associated with winter and the north is Bear. Bear's spirit strengths are power, healing, and intuition. Bear is very nurturing and acts as a protector, helping you to stand your ground. We all know the ferocity of a mother bear. Bear has great strength and can help you connect with your primal power. Bear knows the plants and herbs of the forest and can assist in healing.

The Great Bear also refers to the constellation of Ursa Major (the Big Dipper). Ursa Major helps you find Polaris, the North Star, in the night sky. Polaris is the brightest star of the constellation Ursa Minor (the Little Bear or Little Dipper). The two stars of the cup of the Big Dipper point to Polaris in Ursa Minor. Polaris marks due north and does not appear to move at all. All the stars seem to move around it. This is why Polaris is called the North Star. Polaris has helped people find their way for generations. The Great Bear, Ursa Major, guides you to find Polaris, the North Star. In similar fashion, Bear helps you connect with your north star, the guiding light of your intuition, values, and instinct.

Journal Questions

Where in your life would you benefit from the primal power that Bear offers?

What is your north star, your guide in the darkness?

What does Bear have to teach you?

The Tree of Winter

The tree I associate with winter is the spruce. Spruce is a conifer—it produces seeds from cones, not flowers. It is evergreen, never shedding its needle-like leaves. Spruce teaches us that there are many ways to survive. It takes a path that is different from trees that lose their leaves in the autumn. Spruce can carry heavy snow and provides food and shelter for animals in the cold winter. Spruce offers the qualities of protection, healing, and abundance, and a sense of well-being and feeling grounded. The evergreen is a beacon of hope because its green branches are a visual reminder that life prevails even in the heart of winter. Evergreens are symbols of peace and wisdom.

Journal Questions

What feelings does winter bring up for you?

Where do you find comfort in the depths of winter?

What does an evergreen symbolize for you?

Winter Solstice

Northern Hemisphere: December 21/22

Southern Hemisphere: June 21/22

At the winter solstice the sun has faded into the cold dark of the longest night. You are in the season of waiting, the season of winter. In the darkness, you find peace and stillness, a quiet your soul longs for. Nature rests and invites you to do the same. It is time to listen to your dreams and inner vision. From the darkness, the formless takes form. It is the well of creation and inspiration. Feel the place of winter, of darkness. Through the long dark months of winter, you hold the promise of light within you. This is the longest night, but you know the sun is reborn. The winter solstice marks the return of the light and the beginning of the new year.

Journal Questions

Do you find peace in the deep stillness of winter?

What is your inner vision calling you to create?

How can you honour the rebirth of the light in the heart of winter?

Your Personal Correspondences

Continue to record your observations of how Nature changes through this season.

Walk outside in the snow or cold, then sit in silence beside a fire or in the warmth of your home.

Carry a pebble in your pocket—a stone to represent the strength and stability of the Earth so that you feel grounded and connected each day. (Remember to ask the stone for permission.)

Watch the moon rise or stand out under a full moon.

What animal or tree is symbolic of winter for you?

You may want to consider collecting a gift from Nature for your sacred gift box that is a symbol of winter.

Honouring the Season of Winter

- Decorate an evergreen tree or an artificial tree for the holiday or bring fresh fir, cedar, or spruce boughs into your home.

- Place a wreath on your front door.

- Place a white candle on your table or windowsill.

- Offer bird seed or suet to the animals to share your abundance.

- Donate to a food bank.

- Engage in a quiet meditation.

- Learn about bears.

- Make a snow angel.

- Observe the winter solstice and celebrate the return of the sun by gathering your friends and family for a feast.

May you receive the blessings of winter, of Earth and contemplation.

HEALING NEGATIVE ASSOCIATIONS WITH THE SEASONS

As you connect with the spirit of the seasons, you can heal any potential negative associations you may have. Some people don't like the autumn and winter, for example. The weather can make us feel sad or depressed. Some people don't like the wind; they brace against it.

By connecting with the gifts and wisdom of each season, you can transform your experience, so you are not affected by the weather but move in rhythm with the season, actively searching out the positive qualities that support you.

The seasons offer wisdom, energy, and guidance. Every single day offers you the opportunity to connect with Nature and deepen your understanding of the world you live in. Moving in rhythm with life on Earth can help you navigate your life's terrain and promote a greater sense of well-being. When you offer your heart and hands to Nature, you receive blessings in return, and the whole world moves towards wholeness.

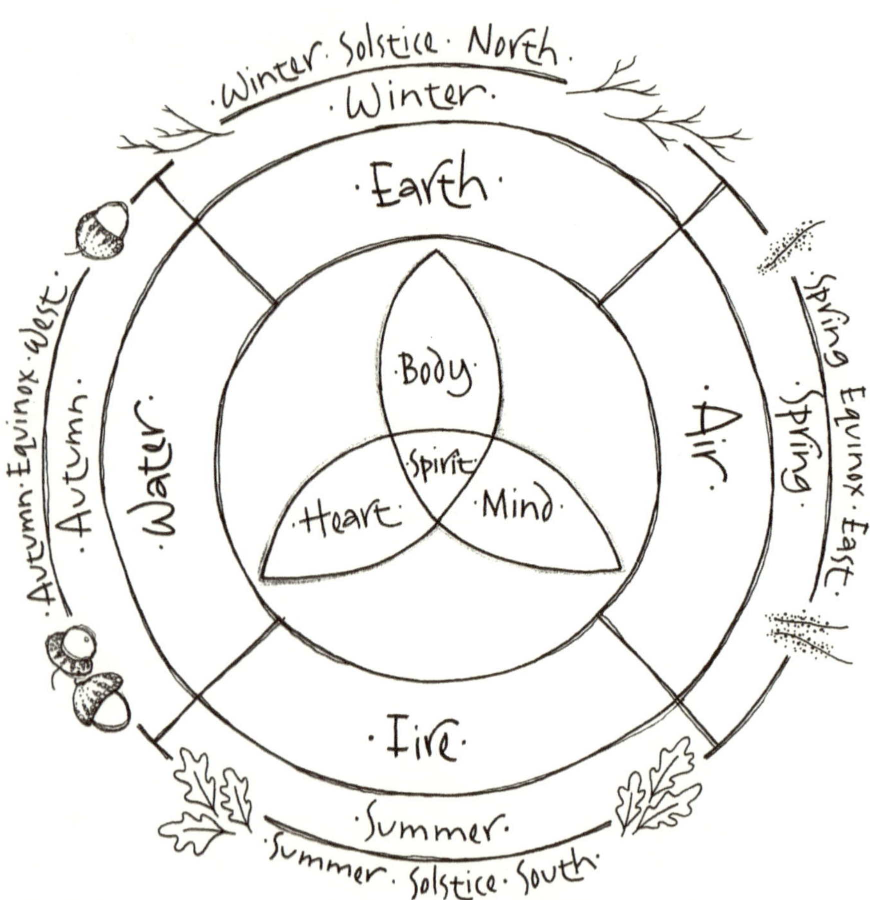

·Seasonal·Solar·Wheel·
·Winter·Solstice·North·
·Winter·
Earth·
·Autumn·Equinox·West·
·Autumn·
Water·
Body
Spirit
·Heart·
·Mind·
Air·
Spring Equinox East·
·Spring·
·Fire·
·Summer·
·Summer·Solstice·South·
·T·HAYDEN·22·

Chapter Six: A Spiritual Practice

CONNECTING WITH THE SACRED

THE IDEA BEHIND A spiritual practice is to create a special time for yourself when you consciously choose to engage with your inner knowing and with the Divine. In doing so, you access your spiritual power and step into the flow of consciousness that is Divine Spirit. A spiritual practice creates a safe and sacred space where you can access your inner wisdom and receive insight, guidance, strength, and blessings. It is an opportunity to step out of your usual way of thinking and just be. Your spiritual practice may be simple or more ritualistic. It is entirely up to you. It's meant to be a gift to yourself to help you remember to be quiet and listen deeply. As time passes, you may find this way of being flows into everything you do. Over time, it may begin to feel like every moment is sacred and your life itself is the spiritual practice.

This book has been about spending time in Nature as a spiritual practice. I recommend that you go outside every day—rain or shine, summer or winter—to receive the blessings of Nature and to offer your appreciation for these blessings. Just going out and paying attention to the beauty around you can change your life. The beauty in Nature can heal you, inspire you, and open a gateway to your inner wisdom, the wisdom of the Earth, and Divine connection. Being in direct contact with Nature is a spiritual practice. Any of the methods discussed so far in this book could serve as a spiritual practice for you.

Your practice may be walking in Nature, sitting with your cat in the morning, or writing in your journal. It may be prayer, meditation, or visiting your tree spirit guide. It may be spent singing, walking a labyrinth, or drumming. Anything can become a spiritual practice if you do it with the intention to connect to the sacred and be fully present to what you are doing. Use your imagination. Listen to your heart. Choose something that has meaning for you and allows you to feel a sacred connection with life.

A spiritual practice is not meant to be an obligation or an additional task to check off your daily list. It is intended to bring you peace and joy, to replenish and empower you. It is a practice of authenticity, connection, and communion with your inner knowing and with the greater life of Spirit. The beauty of a spiritual practice is that it is not only for your personal benefit, but for the benefit of all beings. A practice creates relationship, and relationships sustain life. It is an honouring of your life and of all life.

A morning practice helps you set an intention for the day. My morning practice helps me enter my day with a sense of calm and greater clarity about what is important for me. It allows me to feel the loving support of my helping spirits and to feel gratitude for my life and the beauty around me. Most days I do the Grounded Flow practice, sing my morning song, and offer prayers of gratitude. My morning practice helps me greet each day with new eyes. Like walking in Nature, it helps me gain a new perspective. If my life feels stormy, I find the deep calm beneath the waves, and my day just goes smoother. If I am full of joy, my morning practice helps me to expand into gratitude and appreciation. My morning practice offers a fresh vision and new possibilities. It helps me to live from the deep well of my soul.

An evening practice offers the opportunity to reflect on the day and to be grateful for all that you received. Counting your blessings will leave you with a deep sense of gratitude. I often light a candle or use a chime as part of my evening practice; both are ways to mark the time as sacred. You may wish to spend the time writing in your journal, standing under the moonlight, watching a sunset, or in prayer or meditation. You may want to enter a state of stillness. This is a lovely way to quiet the body and the mind and prepare for sleep. It leaves you feeling calm and peaceful.

It's useful to have a regular spiritual practice, but you don't have to limit yourself to particular times. Stopping, taking a few deep breaths, and connecting with the life within and without is a spiritual practice you can do any time.

CREATING YOUR OWN ALTAR

It is beneficial to have a special place in your home where you can write, pray, meditate, and engage in your spiritual practice or in quiet reflection. This is your sacred space. A sacred space in the physical world is a place where you feel safe and nurtured and where you will not be disturbed. It becomes the physical container for your spiritual practice.

You may also wish to create an altar in your home. Place it in your sacred space as a symbol of Nature, your life, and the seen and unseen worlds. Your altar is a symbol of harmony and balance. It is a physical reminder that the oneness of Spirit underlies all things.

Creating an altar can be as simple as finding four stones to stand for the cardinal directions and placing a candle in the centre of them to represent Spirit. It is customary to place items on the altar that represent the different elements: feathers for Air, crystals, rocks or soil for Earth, a small candle for Fire, and shells for Water, for example. In the teachings I follow, Earth sits in the north, Air in the east, Fire in the south, and Water in the west. You can use a compass to properly orient the directions on your altar. Place your sacred gift box on your altar from time to time to charge it with the feel of the sacred space.

You can set up your altar on the floor, or on a table, or some other surface. You may want to have a special cloth that you can cover the altar with when you are not using it.

Spend time at your altar each day. Pray, meditate, or simply reflect on the elements or the season you are in. It is a focal point for connection to Spirit and to the rhythms of Nature and the Seasonal Solar Wheel.

CEREMONY

Ceremony engages your body, mind, and spirit. It puts you on notice that you are doing something different. Ceremony creates a sacred space and time, allowing you to work beyond your physical senses by moving you from your outer world to your inner world. It creates a vessel to work with Spirit. It is a place where you can trust in the presence of Spirit and access guidance and inspiration. Ceremony works and moves through you at a level beyond your thinking mind.

Ceremony connects you with your inner self. This self is what will carry you through challenges. We often try to figure life out, to get through difficulties with the power of our body, mind, or will. Ceremony helps connect you with the truth of who you are, with your highest self, so that you can live empowered and guided by Spirit. Connecting with your inner self, with your intuition, creates a conversation with Spirit.

Creating ceremonial sacred space involves the combination of your intention and a ritual act to connect you to Spirit. You may say a prayer, light a candle, burn incense, or sound a chime to create a sacred space. This space is for you to do your spiritual work, to pray and meditate, to journal and reflect. It is a place to feel held, protected, and deeply loved. It may be helpful to think of this space as a circle of energy around you. It is about consciously setting a clear intention to connect with the more profound wisdom within you and with Divine wisdom. Ceremony helps us to be our best self and to receive the blessings of the sacred in our life.

Aspects of Ceremony

There are certain universal aspects of ceremony. Ceremony has a beginning or opening, a middle, and an end or closing. Ceremony is held in sacred space that has been cleared and blessed. Ceremony calls in the Divine and your helping spirits and has a specific intention. Ceremony begins and ends with gratitude for the guidance, inspiration, protection, and support you have received and closes with a request for peace, love, and blessings for all life. The following is an example of a basic ceremony structure that you can adapt for your own use.

Opening the Circle

Breathe deeply until you feel calm and peaceful.

Imagine a circle of light around you. The circle of light is the container for your sacred space. You stand at the centre of this circle with Divine Source and can connect with all life in the circle.

Say a prayer. Ask that your circle be safe and clear. You may wish to light a candle, sprinkle water, or burn incense or herbs to ritually cleanse the circle. If it feels right, sound a chime to mark the beginning of the ceremony.

Give thanks for the day and pray for blessing and guidance.

Call in Divine Spirit and your helping spirits. Your helping spirits are beings of compassion and respect who always have your highest good and the highest good of all life in mind. Ask for their guidance and protection during the ceremony. Give thanks for their presence.

I like to call in the spirits of the directions and the elements, and I invite each one in turn. A calling-in does not mean there is a separation from you and Spirit or from the energies of the directions or elements. The elements and directions are always present, within and without. An invocation is more of an acknowledgment of their presence and an intention to receive and work with them. It is an opportunity to welcome them into your circle and ceremony.

You can call in any helping spirit. You may want to call in helping spirits to whom you have a special connection, like an animal spirit guide or your power animal. It is good to set the intention that only those beings who are benevolent and compassionate, be allowed in your circle.

Stating your Intention

You can set an intention to ask for help or guidance with a specific challenge or concern in your life, to receive whatever information, energy, or guidance is best for you in that moment, or to ask for Divine blessings on a situation or action. When setting intention, always include, "if it is in my highest good and the good of all life." This caveat allows for the reality that we may not know what is in our highest good, (even if we think we do!) ensures no harm is done to any being and allows for unexpected blessings to come to us.

Middle Ceremony

What you do as the main action of the ceremony is entirely up to you. You might sit quietly and gaze at the candle flame. You might pick up your journal and let the words flow from Spirit to page. You might do nothing but breathe. You may choose to connect with and receive from a particular element or direction. Use your imagination and do what you feel called to do. Enter ceremony with no expectation of what information you will receive. Just be quiet and listen. Sometimes intuitive guidance and understanding comes right away, and sometimes it comes over time.

Ending the Ceremony

When your time in ceremony feels complete, take three deep breaths to feel calm and centred. Offer thanks for the wisdom, guidance, and inspiration you have received. Thank your helping spirits, the spirits of the directions and elements, and Divine Spirit.

When you are ready, release the circle with a prayer of gratitude and wish peace and blessings for all life. Blow out the candles. Take a moment to wiggle your fingers and toes to ensure you are entirely in your body after your ceremony. Having a bite to eat is an excellent way to ground yourself in your body and be fully present in the here and now. Be sure to drink plenty of water. Take a few moments to write in your journal or to reflect on the experience, and then carry the energy of the ceremony—the energy of peace, love, and gratitude—with you into your day or evening. You may wish to offer a physical gift to Spirit in the form of herbs, water, or flowers. These items may be placed at the base of a tree or sprinkled to the wind. Be sure to offer only natural or biodegradable gifts.

The above example illustrates the basic structure of a ceremony that you can adapt to your personal intentions and needs. Listen deeply to your helping spirits and your inner knowing, and you will learn how to create ceremony for yourself. You can create a ceremony for your spiritual practice or use ceremony when you wish to explore an issue, deepen a relationship with a helping spirit, mark an occasion, or offer gratitude.

Things to Consider

Always engage in ceremony when you feel calm. If you do not feel relaxed or balanced, go directly to Nature instead. Being in direct contact with Nature will help you find calm and stability. It is best to do ceremony within a circle of light as it creates an energetic boundary, a safe and sacred container for your work. You may choose to use the Grounded Flow practice to open your ceremony.

If at any time during ceremony you begin to feel uncomfortable or disoriented, please know that you can stop and close the ceremony whenever it feels right to you. Trust your own knowing.

Always take any messages or visions you receive with a grain of salt. Look at it through the lens of your common sense. Messages may come from your inner knowing or they may arise from your thinking mind. Ask yourself if the message aligns with your ethics and values. Does it have a practical application in your life? Does it feel right? Over time, you will be able to discern if the feeling or thought has arisen from your intuition or from your thinking mind. Intuition has a ring of truth to it. It resonates. There is no need to explain or justify it—you just know. You feel it in your body.

Your helping spirits will never direct you to do anything that would harm you or another. They are always positive and loving. If you receive any unhelpful message, stop what you are doing and disregard it.

Nature, meditation, and ceremony are spaces where we can access our inner knowing and intuition. When we are still and listen deeply, we can uncover pain or emotion—in the body or in our internal emotional landscape—that we have buried or ignored. This can be hard. I encourage you to acknowledge any pain, emotion, or negative thought that arises, but not dwell on it. Acknowledge it, feel it, and release it to Spirit, shifting your focus to loving-kindness for yourself, for another, or for the situation. Release the pain to Spirit and immerse yourself in light. Seek help from a doctor or other professional if that feels right.

We do not command Nature or the elements or try to direct them through our will. Our intention is to develop a loving and respectful relationship with the Earth and with the helping spirits. As a Druid, I take responsibility for my actions and intentions. I work with the flow of life and have respect for all life. The sacred ceremonial circle is never intended to coerce or force.

Only engage in ceremony on behalf of yourself. Do not do ceremony on behalf of others unless you have their explicit permission and an exact intention. It is a soul violation to assume you know what is best for someone else.

LIVING INTENTIONALLY

Creating sacred space through ceremony is a way to slow down and live intentionally. When you are quiet and listen deeply, you access your inner knowing and intuition. You discover an awareness within you that you may not have realized existed. This space invites you to feel what you may not want to feel, to see and address what you need to look at in a safe and protected place.

Ceremony can allow you to release your burdens and to access wisdom and guidance that is beyond your thinking mind. You can access your own understanding and the ancient knowledge that lives within and around you. You invite the sacred into your everyday living. Ceremony helps foster your relationship with Spirit and your inner knowing. By fostering that relationship, you nourish yourself and all the world around you.

You can use ceremony for many different things: for the beginning or ending of a work project, a creative endeavour, or a trip. You can use ceremony for a life transition, such as marriage, divorce, or the birth of a child. It is an opportunity to pay attention to your body, to your inner guidance, and to connect with the Spirit that infuses all.

Everything you do can become a spiritual practice if you pay attention and hold an awareness of the sacred in all things. Not everything needs to be done in the container of a ceremony. While you are out walking in the heart of the city, you can always notice the Sky or feel the Earth beneath your feet. Making dinner can become a spiritual practice if you are present and aware and feel gratitude for the Spirit of the plants or animals you are receiving nourishment from. Pay attention, be present, listen, acknowledge, and be in gratitude. Your whole life will be a spiritual practice.

The Transformative Power of a Fire Ceremony

The flames dance and swirl, reaching skyward. Flickers of blue and green appear from the orange glow. Bright sparks ascend to the heavens, lifted by the flames. A steady warmth radiates from the Fire, bathing us in its light.

Humans have gathered around Fire for thousands of years. Fire offers us light and warmth, cooks our food, heats our homes, and nourishes our Spirit. It keeps our fears at bay on the darkest of nights. Fire is central to our existence. The hearth is the heart of every home.

Fire is an element that can create all kinds of feelings. We all love to sit around a campfire, mesmerized by its beauty and power. We have all been burned by Fire at some point too.

Fire is a symbol of transformation. Fire creates, transforms, destroys, and renews. It is a living symbol of the cycle of birth, death, and rebirth that we experience on many levels in our own lives. We see this cycle repeated with the birth and death of our physical bodies, with the changing seasons, and with each sunrise and sunset.

We can partner with the spirit of Fire to invoke enthusiasm and energy, for purification, and for healing and renewal. Fire illuminates our hearts, ignites our passions, and nourishes our body and soul. Fire releases our burdens, transforming old beliefs and patterns to ash and transmuting their energy to the purest level of divine light. We can use the Fire of our experience to create positive change in our lives.

In a Fire ceremony, we connect with the spirit of Fire and the Divine Source that underlies all that is. We approach Fire as a partner, with respect and gratitude, and release to the Fire our limiting beliefs, stories, doubts, and fears—all that does not serve us anymore. We ask Fire to transform the energy of those feelings and thoughts into new light and power. We receive this new, creative, life-giving energy to inspire new growth in our lives. Fire carries our intentions and prayers to the world of Spirit. The spirit of Fire offers transformation and healing light.

Preparation

Fire is an element that we can make, which heightens our responsibility. It is powerful, and you need to feel safe and comfortable working with it. Follow proper fire safety and techniques when working with a flame. Never leave a candle or campfire unattended. Be sure you have a safe place or container. A Fire ceremony is best held outside. If that is not possible, try placing a candle in a fireproof bowl filled with sand and work in a sink or bathtub where water is handy. If you do not feel comfortable working with Fire, don't. Whether you are working outside or inside, have a pen and paper ready—you will need them during the ceremony.

Only burn natural fibres or paper. Do not burn anything that is made of plastic or is not biodegradable.

Items

- Burning bowl, sand and candle, fireplace, or outdoor firepit

- Water at the ready

- Pen and paper

- Journal

- Dried herbs, like juniper or mugwort, or an herb of your choice

Opening

Light your Fire or candle. The candle is at the center of your circle.

Breathe deeply in and out three times. Feel yourself grounded on the Earth. Feel the energy of the Earth flowing up into you through the soles of your feet. Then feel the power of the Sky flowing down through the top of your head. Imagine this energy filtering and clearing all aspects of your being, which includes a space of three to six feet around you, with the candle in the center. Imagine this circle cleansed of intrusive energy, of any thoughts, feelings, and energy that do not align with who you are. The circle is cleared and then filled with the highest level of divine light. Imagine this light forming a circle of protection, a sacred and safe space around you. You may wish to pray, asking for divine guidance and offering gratitude to the spirit of Fire.

State your intention to work with the spirit of Fire to heal and transform your life.

Release

The first aspect of the ceremony is releasing that which no longer serves you, whether it is a feeling, a belief, or a behaviour. Even if you can't name it, you can release it to be transformed by the Fire.

Write down all that you wish to give to the Fire, everything you want to release and heal—your stories, your beliefs, your pain, your sorrow, your rage. Use individual slips of paper for each thing you give to the fire or, if it feels right, write a letter. Our thoughts and our words have power. They carry an energy, a vibration. When you are ready, feel the words within your heart. Place the paper into the flames (if you have written a letter, roll it up loosely). Watch as the Fire burns it all away. (If you cannot safely burn your paper, soak the paper in water and bury it in the Earth.)

The element of Fire holds within it the power of the sun, of growth and abundance. Fire can renew, heal, purify, destroy, and create. New life arises from its ashes.

Receive

In the second part of the ceremony, you receive energy from the spirit of Fire. When you let go of all that does not serve you, you create a space for new energy to enter. Hold your palms out to the flame. Receive the warmth and light of the fire. Imagine new energy and light of the highest vibration gently flowing into your heart. Feel the light flow into every aspect of your being. Every cell in your body is alive with light.

Closing

When you feel complete, say a prayer of gratitude to the Fire. You may wish to offer a dried herb or flower to the Fire to thank and bless it for its help.

Take three breaths. Feel yourself grounded and centred in your body and on the Earth. Give thanks to Fire and Divine Spirit for their help and guidance in your ceremony. You may wish to speak the following words aloud:

A flame is lit in the depths of my soul.

With the light comes new understanding, new awareness, and new beginnings.

May the light illuminate my heart, and may my heart illuminate the world.

May I be surrounded by love and light.

Peace and blessings to all.

Imagine the circle of light you created at the beginning dissolving. Then imagine all the energies you called into it flowing out to the world in a manner that is for the highest good of all life.

Your Fire ceremony is complete. You may wish to record your experience in your journal with words, drawings, or with paint or coloured markers. When you are ready, be sure to extinguish the Fire completely. May your Fire ceremony bring you renewal and power.

Final Words

NATURE SPEAKS TO YOU. All you need do is listen. It is in the whisper of the wind, the rushing river, and the warmth of the sun. A respectful relationship with Nature offers peace, joy, inspiration, and guidance.

Nature is calling you to remember your ancient connection and your sacred place in the circle. When you root yourself, like a tree, in the ancient wisdom of the Earth, you can access strength and stability and feel energized and renewed.

Nature can be the source of your most profound learning. It can guide you in your daily living and bring you home to your inner knowing. The natural world enables you to access the wisdom of your heart and of Spirit.

Nature helps you to be in relationship with yourself and with the other beings on the planet. There is harmony, a grounded flow, when you are in a relationship with Nature. Life becomes filled with possibilities, wonder, and beauty. You understand that a tree is more than a tree, that the animals and plants, the stars and the stones, all have their own teachings. With every sunrise, your heart and the heart of the Earth beat as one.

Listen to the heart of Nature. Nature brings you back into your body, into your heart, and into your feelings. In the quiet, you can hear the wisdom that lives within you and around you. You can be reborn in Nature. I believe in the healing power of Nature, and I know that as you heal yourself, you heal the world around you.

As you build relationship with Nature, with your inner self, and with Spirit, you heal and grow, and you increase your ability to love and care for others and the world around you. This is a personal path, but it is not a selfish one.

It is my sincere hope that you have deepened your relationship with Nature through the experiences offered in this book. As we grow in love and respect for Nature, we cannot help but be worried and fear for her future. We see the cutting down of forests, the ever-encroaching building on the land, the pollution of the air, soil, and water, the mass killing of animals, the loss of habitat for the wild ones. We see that the ecosystems all life depends on are compromised and under pressure. We may feel rage and despair as we live through the experience of climate change, drought, fires, floods, and food shortages on a global scale.

It is easy to feel overwhelmed. The problems seem insurmountable. But know this—Nature is capable of tremendous healing and will rebalance herself.

What can you do to help Nature rebalance? Change begins with the individual, with your choices and behaviours. Look into your heart and see what you can do to support the Earth. What can you stop doing or start doing that would help heal the Earth? Enter ceremony or meditation and ask what the Earth needs from you. How can you care for the natural world? It might be by recycling, composting, and supporting reforestation projects, community gardening, or animal welfare. It might be by helping to change legislation to offer more protection of the environment or by raising awareness. It might be by being mindful of what you buy, what you eat, and how you live.

Whatever path you take to begin healing the Earth, I know it begins with a deep and abiding love and respect for Nature. Pay attention and be grateful. A tree gave its life for the paper in your hand. Remember you receive gifts of abundance from the Earth and the Divine. Love the Earth, love yourself, and live your values. Treat all life with honour and respect. Give thanks to the plants and animals, the wind and water, the Earth and the Sun for the gifts you receive. What we give, we receive. Offer love, not judgment. Hope, not despair. Peace, not violence. You receive so many gifts and blessings from all aspects of Nature. Honour and acknowledge these gifts. Listen to Nature and your inner wisdom and you will know what action is right for you. You can change the world. Change begins with you.

Go Outside.

Breathe.

Listen.

Nature will show you the way.

Nature is the path home.

Journal Entry: A Summer Storm

We ride our horses in single file on the trail, weaving through the trees on a narrow path. The forest gleams a thousand shades of green in the dull grey light. Rain pours from the leaden skies, pattering my helmet and coat. Water runs down my horses back, trickling into my boots, and soaking my socks. The rain falls, muffling the sounds of the horses' hooves on the soft Earth.

Flashes of lightning and booming thunder accompany our every step, yet the feeling that envelops us is one of peace, not disquiet. The horses are not bothered by the storm. They know about the rain and thunder and are intimate with the elements in a way that I can only imagine.

The peace of the trees flows into me, carrying with it a timeless strength and grace. I can feel the presence of the mountains, rocky sentinels, watching our passage. All my senses are alive. I am aware of the call of the loon and the sighing of the wind in the trees. I listen to the rolling thunder and the rush of the river. The song of the trees flows around me. The trees sing with voices that I cannot hear with my ears, but I feel with my heart. Their voices lift me up and soothe me.

The forest has a wild abundance of life and possibility. Both the known and the unknowable are here. There is an intersection of the visible and invisible. I see the trees and know that I am only encountering a small part of the being that is the tree. When you look at the forest, the forest looks back at you. The woods teem with animals, yet they are elusive and hidden. I know that bears, cougars, and wolves all live in this realm. Although we do not encounter them face to face, we can sense them on the periphery of our vision, dancing in the shadows. The soul is like that, shy and elusive, camouflaged by our roles and responsibilities. The forest beckons the hidden aspects of our being to come forward, offering us a glimpse of an unrealized truth, opening our hearts to a new understanding of ourselves.

I am part of All That Is, awake and alive, so far from the busyness of my everyday life. All my tasks and goals fall away, reshaped by the wonder of this moment. The sharp painful edges of my life are smoothed over, softened into something malleable.

It is a gift to be here at this moment, without judgment, without worry, without what-ifs or what is next. There is only now. Nature offers a new perspective and healing.

It is as though I have stepped through a portal to a different world where feeling is the stuff of life, where we all breathe as One—horses, people, rain, and trees. With each step, my horse carries me deeper into this lucid dream, awakening senses and aspects of myself that I didn't even know were there.

This awareness is the magic of Nature.

This knowing is grace.

This feeling is love.

It is a blessing to move in rhythm with my heart and the heart of life.

I carry this memory with me as a talisman and a guide. *

A Blessing for You

May you be blessed with a summer storm in the wildwood.

May the rain wash away all the noise and confusion.

May Nature show you the truth of who you are.

May you breathe as one with the Earth.

I wish you joy and wonder on your journey home.

Peace and blessings of Nature to you,

Jan

Acknowledgements

I acknowledge that I live on the traditional territories of the Blackfoot Confederacy, including the Siksika, Piikani, and Kainai Nations. I would also like to acknowledge the territory of Treaty Seven, that is also home to the Tsuut'ina Nation and the Stoney Nakoda First Nations of Bearspaw, Chiniki, and Wesley, and the Métis Nation-Region 3, and all the Indigenous and non-Indigenous people who make their homes in the Treaty 7 region of Southern Alberta.

I acknowledge all the many First Nations, Métis, and Inuit whose footsteps have marked these lands for centuries.

This land acknowledgment was received with gratitude from Tarra Wright Many Chief.

Seasonal Solar Wheel Illustration. Concept: Jan Hornford. Design and Illustration: Tara Hayden.

A special thank you to my initial editor, Alex Rettie, for his patience, thoughtful comments, and kindness, and to everyone at Friesen Press.

An asterisk references material that first appeared in articles I wrote for Soulbridging.com. Modified. Used with permission.

I would like to thank:

Divine Spirit

My family

Smoke and Sir Henry

My helping spirits and guides

My mentors: Mona Wind, Vickie Tait, and Manfred Lukas

The Order of Bards, Ovates, and Druids

Mother Earth

All trees—my strength and stay, my joy

Bright Blessings!

Tips for Day Hikes in Wilderness Areas

1. Tell someone where you are going and when you expect to return. Tell them what action they should take if you are late.

2. Buy or download a topographic map of where you are going. It's good to have a detailed map of your terrain.

3. Carry a compass.

4. Check the weather conditions.

5. Be aware of any natural hazards in the area (ticks, bears, trail closures, etc.).

6. Carry at least one litre of water.

7. Bring food. High energy snacks like trail mix, nuts, fruit, and energy bars are best.

8. Wear layers of clothing, including wool or synthetic sweater, scarf, rain jacket, warm hat, gloves, and a sun hat.

9. Wear footwear suitable for the terrain.

10. Carry a small first aid kit that includes moleskin for blisters.

11. Bring sunscreen and insect repellant.

12. Bring a multipurpose tool.

13. Bring a lighter.

14. Bring a headlamp.

15. Bring toilet paper, hand sanitizer, and small plastic baggies to carry any used tissue out with you.

16. Optional: Bring a small foam pad to sit on as it will keep you clean, warm, and dry.

17. Bring your journal and a pen.

Please do not pick flowers. Only remove natural objects like pinecones, twigs or stones from the environment, and only with permission from Nature. Please take out everything that you brought in with you. Don't litter. Be respectful of Nature and leave everything as you found it.

Bibliography

Andrews, Ted. *Animal Speak*. Woodbury, MN: Llewellyn Publications, 2007.

Billington, Penny. *The Path of Druidry*. Woodbury, MN: Llewellyn Publications, 2011.

Carr-Gomm, Philip. *Druid Mysteries*. London: Rider 2002.

_______________. *The Druid Way*. London: Element, 1993.

Deatsman, Colleen, and Paul Bowersox. *Seeing in the Dark*. San Francisco: Red Wheel/Weiser, LLC, 2009.

Endredy, James. *Earthwalks for Body and Spirit*. Rochester, VT: Bear and Company, 2002.

Freeman, Mara. *Kindling the Celtic Spirit*. New York: Harper One, 2000.

Ingerman, Sandra. *Walking in Light*. Boulder, CO: Sounds True, 2014.

Karoway, Natalia. *Living Sacred Ceremony*. Sweet & Sacred, 2015.

Kimmerer, Robin Wall. *Braiding Sweetgrass*. Minneapolis: Milkweed Editions, 2013.

Kynes, Sandra. *Whispers from the Woods*. Woodbury, MN: Llewellyn Publications, 2006.

Matthews, Caitlin. *Singing the Soul Back Home*. London: Eddison Books Limited, 2018.

Restall Orr, Emma. *Druidry*. London: Thorsons, 2000.

Wagamese, Richard. *One Drum*. Madeira Park, BC: Douglas &
     McIntrye, 2019.

_______________. *Embers*. Madeira Park, BC: Douglas & McIntyre, 2016.

Jan has walked a nature based spiritual path for many years. In addition to being a full Druid member of the Order of Bards, Ovates, and Druids, Jan holds a BSc Honours degree in zoology, has studied with Shaman Manfred Lukas, and is a Certified Retreat Coach and Labyrinth Facilitator. Jan offers a blend of knowledge and experience to help people connect with Nature through her writing, drum circles, labyrinth walks, and retreats. She empowers individuals to discover the earth's wisdom, finding guidance, meaning, and inspiration for a more fulfilling life.

janhornford.com